Faith Based

GEOGRAPHIES OF JUSTICE AND SOCIAL TRANSFORMATION

Faith Based

RELIGIOUS NEOLIBERALISM AND THE POLITICS OF WELFARE IN THE UNITED STATES

JASON HACKWORTH

THE UNIVERSITY OF GEORGIA PRESS
Athens & London

Athens, Georgia 30602
www.ugapress.org

Designed by Walton Harris
Set in 10/13 Minion Pro

Printed digitally in the United States of America

Library of Congress Cataloging-in-Publication Data

Hackworth, Jason R.
Faith based : religious neoliberalism and the politics of welfare in the United States / Jason Hackworth.
p. cm. — (Geographies of justice and social transformation ; 11)
Includes bibliographical references and index.
ISBN-13: 978-0-8203-4303-7 (hardcover : alk. paper)
ISBN-10: 0-8203-4303-X (hardcover : alk. paper)
ISBN-13: 978-0-8203-4304-4 (pbk. : alk. paper)
ISBN-10: 0-8203-4304-8 (pbk. : alk. paper)
1. Neoliberalism—United States—History. 2. Religious right—United States—History. 3. Conservatism—United States—History. I. Title.
JC574.2.U6H33 2012
361.973—dc23 2011043748

British Library Cataloging-in-Publication Data available

CONTENTS

PREFACE

I sometimes pine to be a historian. My job would then consist of excavating fragments of the past and debating with my colleagues about whose interpretation or archival source is correct. The historical event in question wouldn't change, but the light we might shed on it could — or at least that's my romanticized version of a historian's life. Instead, I foolishly chose to become a geographer — a political economist really — with an interest in current political events in the United States. I love thinking about such issues and bringing social science methods and theory to bear to prod the conversation surrounding them. The only problem is that with academic publishing time horizons, it is almost impossible to publish anything except yesterday's news. By the time that you analyze the data, write the paper (or book), wait for the reviews, and publish, it is almost inevitably old news.

What follows is an attempt, perhaps foolish, to wade into another current event. The book is about the synergies and tensions between economic and religious conservatives in the United States. When I first began thinking about this topic in early 2005, the U.S. political landscape was very different from how it is today. The Bush administration's faith-based initiative was heating up again after years of being dormant, and the Religious Right seemed in control of the political sphere like no other group. In one stretch that stands out to many students of this subject, politicians were tripping over themselves to nullify the decision by a brain-dead Florida woman's husband to remove her from life support in March 2005. A few months later and a few hundred miles away in New Orleans, many in that same group stood by and waited for (largely religious) charities to come to the rescue of a city that was literally drowning. It was hard not to conclude that their efforts were specifically designed to impress the Religious Right.

But then 2006 happened and the Republicans were rebuked in part for both episodes. And then 2008 happened. Barack Obama was elected and the Religious Right seemed relegated to the background for at least a moment, if not for good. It would have been easy to say, "It's time to move on; this topic has expired," and to be honest, I contemplated doing so. The Religious Right, after a series of scandals, seemed to lose its political teeth, and the scale of the problems facing the new administration in 2009 seemed too grand to rely on religious charities or hollow political stunts to resolve. The first few legislative initiatives of the Obama administration seemed to confirm this shift. The stimulus bill, financial regulation, and the health care act all seemed to foreground the role of government and to background the ideal of religious charities and other civil society intermediaries to solve the pressing problems of the day.

By 2010, the political landscape had changed yet again in a fairly fundamental way. The Tea Party had grown in power and ushered in the largest shift of House seats to the Republicans since the Great Depression. The mantra of "less government" seemed to have regained its cachet after several years of ringing anachronistic. While the public face of the Tea Party has been steadfastly oriented around antiseptic budgetary items like "balancing the budget" and "reducing government waste," a recent Pew Poll found that many in the Tea Party were not only devout Christians but also relied on that faith for guidance in politics. Journalists have revealed, moreover, that many of the key Religious Right activists of the 1990s have reinvented themselves as Tea Party organizers in the post-Obama era. What are we to make of this? Is this the last gasp of a discredited Religious Right or a precursor to a time when politicians trip over themselves again to impress them? To be honest, I do not know—not now anyway, in the summer of 2011 when this is being written—but I hope that this book can both help start a conversation about how we got here and offer a framework for thinking about the next few steps.

This book is about the complicated relationship between neoliberalism and religious conservatism, particularly concerning the theme of welfare. I have been writing about "neoliberalism" for almost ten years now. By neoliberalism, I mean the political movement, derived from "classical liberals" like Adam Smith and John Locke and revived by mid-twentieth-century ideologues like Friedrich Hayek, Milton Friedman, Ayn Rand, and Ludwig von Mises. Definitions abound, but I generally think of it in the following way. First, neoliberalism involves an overwhelming emphasis on the individual. Individuals are responsible and best able to provide for themselves, solve problems alone, and decide what is best for them. Individuals are responsible for their own failures and successes and should be rewarded and punished accordingly. Second, it consists of an almost religious belief that the market (and the vehicle of property) is the best way to promote an individual's choice. And third, it consists of an almost equally religious belief that the state will inhibit both the market and individual choice. Synonyms abound, especially in the United States, where very few people actually self-identify with the label, but I see it as broadly similar to "libertarianism" or "economic conservatism."

It has long been my view that neoliberalism, or whatever we call it, could not exist by itself. Politicians who run on a purely "libertarian" platform rarely get more than a fraction of the vote (especially when the specifics of their intended budget cuts come to light), and they often must cling to more electorally successful strategies like being antiabortion or promilitary to garner enough votes to win in even the most conservative districts. So why has it endured? Why do millions of dollars flow each year to neoliberal think tanks like CATO? Why are mantras like "government isn't the solution; it's the problem" routinely invoked, and why do they successfully resonate with voters no matter what the context? Why is neoliberalism so seductive? It needs, in my view, other political supports to be sustainable. It flourishes, for example, when a crisis occurs or when there is some threat to national sovereignty, when its proponents can demonstrate that it is the best, or "only," way out of a current problem. This book is about the support offered by the Religious Right, and in particular the effect it has had on the realm of welfare. The Religious Right is a polyglot of different agendas, and economic conservatism is generally not a central plank. But the Religious Right has been part of an electoral coalition since 1980, and a self-conscious ideational "fusion" with economic conservatives since at least the 1960s. It has helped win elections, but it has also, in my view, helped soften the edges of cold-hearted bare-knuckled neoliberalism. Saying that welfare should be abolished or that Medicare is unconstitutional sounds a lot more compassionate when you can point to an alternative. This study argues that disparate religiously oriented private institutions with no government funding will never be an actual replacement, but the *notion*, the assertion, that they will, or could, be has gotten a lot of political mileage.

Starting in 2007, I began presenting and publishing excerpts of what would eventually become this book. I thank the publishers for allowing me to reuse, rework, and reprint some of this earlier material. A great deal has been added to it in this book, but bits and pieces have been published previously under the following banners: "Faith in the Neoliberalization of Post-Katrina New Orleans," with Josh Akers, in *Tijdschrift voor Economische en Sociale Geografie 102* (© Blackwell); "Compassionate Neoliberalism?: Evangelical Christianity, the Welfare State, and the Politics of the Right," in *Studies in Political Economy 86*; "Faith, Welfare, and the City: The Mobilization of Religious Organizations for Neoliberal Ends," in *Urban Geography 31*(6), 750–73 (© Bellwether Press, Ltd.,

8640 Guilford Road, Columbia, Md., 21046; reprinted with permission; all rights reserved); "Neoliberalism, Partiality, and the Politics of Faith-Based Welfare in the United States," in *Studies in Political Economy 84*; "Normalizing 'Solutions' to 'Government Failure': Media Representations of Habitat for Humanity," in *Environment and Planning A 41*(11), 2686–705 (2009; © Pion Ltd., London); and "Neoliberalism for God's Sake: Sectarian Justifications for Secular Policy Transformation in the United States," in A. L. Molendijk, J. Beaumont, and C. Jedan (Eds.), *Exploring the Postsecular: The Religious, the Political, the Urban* (Leiden, Netherlands: Brill, 2010).

As this work began to trickle out, the reactions to it began to trickle in. In general, I received two very different responses. From secular political economists (a group with whom I am most familiar as a scholar), I received a reaction that might best be paraphrased as "yes, this is obvious, the Religious Right hates welfare . . . why bother writing this." From scholars of religion, I generally got a very different, often defensive, reaction but one that could be paraphrased as "the story is much more complicated; you don't give enough credit or focus to the social gospel, liberation theology, evangelical compassion, the Black protestant church in the United States, or some other political or theological thread of the Christian experience." Strangely when my critical pen veered toward something theoretical like a critique of Marx or something practical like a critique of welfare, the reaction was entirely opposite . . . but I digress. This reaction surprised me. When I began thinking and writing about religion, I naively assumed that most authors on the topic were basically like me: atheish personally but multicultural enough to find most incarnations of religion interesting in an anthropological sort of way. But I sensed a defensiveness among my religion-scholar colleagues that seemed to belie this. In private conversations where I was able to ask more follow-up questions, several admitted that they bristled at the way that I had, in their view, denigrated the work of faith-motivated antipoverty activists by spending so much time on the most judgmental, most conservative segments of the faith-based social services world. To be honest, I don't know what to do with that sentiment. It is not my intent to alienate religious readers, and for the record, I do not think that religion is motivated only for regressive ends. Clearly it is a powerful force in the lives of many, and sometimes that force manifests itself in progressive ways. But by the same token, it is difficult to ignore the fact that the overwhelming political influence of the Religious Right on the U.S. welfare state in the past forty years has not been a progressive one. Whether the narrow influence of figures like Gary North or the wide influence of figures like Jerry Falwell, when it comes to issues of economic or social welfare, it is more common for self-professed religious leaders in the United States to pray at the feet of Milton Friedman than at those of John Maynard Keynes or Karl Marx. Though it is rarely the centerpiece issue for Religious Right groups, it is difficult for me to conclude that the marginal presence of the social gospel or liberation theology nullifies the antitax, small-government activist successes of more conservative threads of the American evangelical Protestant experience. I think, in short, that religion, particularly organized politically and theologically conservative white Protestantism in the United States, has been a crucial influence promoting and supporting "neoliberalism," particularly with regard to social welfare.

But I do not dismiss the point that my progressive religious counterparts are making outright. In fact, their claim that the religious experience of Christians belies a smooth conflation of fundamentalist theology and neoliberal policies is in many ways an axiom from which I build my argument. The Bible, as many liberation theologians and adherents of the social gospel like to point out, is not at all an unequivocally neoliberal text. In fact, many classical liberals and neoliberals were either irreligious or even atheistic, as in the case of Ayn Rand, because they felt it inspired collectivism. Ayn Rand once famously called Christianity the "kindergarten of socialism" and loathed the Bible's messages of cooperation and sharing. Religious neoliberals, of course, dispute this strenuously and point to an equal number of biblical verses that they say justify neoliberalism (see chapter 2), but the notion that Christianity is smoothly in line with antiwelfarism or antitax policies is debatable to say the least. The success of the fusion of the Religious Right and neoliberalism *politically* is, by contrast, less disputable as it has ushered in a large number of very powerful politicians and influential policies. Herein lies the paradox and the central research question, namely, how (and in what ways), given that the Bible and the larger American Christian experience is less than unequivocal about economic, social justice, and poverty matters, has the overwhelming political synergy supported neoliberalism? Most work on neoliberalism does not really connect these two or consider religion at all. Most work on religion and the welfare state does not really address neoliberalism and the Religious Right's role in promoting it. This book is about that "fusion"—the union of neoliberal and religiously conservative politics—and its influence on the realm of social welfare in particular.

Almost every book is collaborative in some sense, no matter how many authors are listed on the cover, and this project is no different. Any errors, omissions, and faulty reasoning that remain are all mine, but I would like to thank a number of people for their help along the way. Several public presentations of this work were very helpful at workshopping these ideas and sharpening them as they developed. These include the Department of Geography at York University, the Department of Anthropology at Stanford University, the University of Groningen workshop on post-secularity, the Department of Political Science at Columbia University, and the Centre for the Study of the United States here at my home institution, the University of Toronto. I appreciate the invitations but more so the feedback on this work.

A number of individuals have been particularly helpful on this project. Justin Beaumont, Jason Dittmer, and Candice Dias are part of a small but growing group of geographers interested in these issues. I appreciate their advice, friendship, and camaraderie. Conversations and prodding — sometimes directly on this topic, sometimes not — from several people at my university have really helped. These include Ron Buliung, Tenley Conway, Amrita Daniere, Kanishka Goonewardena, Robert Lewis, Katharine Rankin, David Rayside, Matti Siemiatycki, Rachel Silvey, Sarah Wakefield, Alan Walks, and Kathi Wilson. They are certainly my intellectual core and in my opinion the intellectual center of the department where I work. Special thanks in this regard should be reserved for my colleague and friend Matt Farish. Whether the topic is the importance of Grover Norquist to the American Right or the importance of Grover to the Muppets, Matt's fascination with American culture, high and low, has been very helpful for me in developing this project, and pretty funny too. Susan Calanza's unsuccessful efforts at keeping me sane among the insane and Erik Karmol's annual pilgrimage to Toronto are also very much appreciated.

Derek Krisoff, my editor at the University of Georgia, has done a terrific job of managing the review of this manuscript, and Nik Heynen was helpful at getting it off the ground. I very much appreciate their efforts. Mitchell Gray helped a great deal in getting the manuscript into shape through his editorial work. Last but not least, I thank SSHRC, the Canadian Social Sciences and Humanities Research Council, which not only funded part of this project but has continued to indulge my fascination with American politics when there are so many interesting questions to answer in Canada. These funds have gone to pay a number of very helpful research assistants over the years who have been invaluable. They include Josh Akers, Laura Casselman, Paul Grise, Erin Gullikson, Frances Lay, Julie Mah, Alex Miceli, Kirsten Stein, and Sally Turner.

I dedicate this book to two sets of people. First, to my father and mother, Ted and Ann Hackworth. We have very different views about the role of government in society, but we agree on the value of education. I appreciate both of them very much for insisting on that for me and my siblings. Second, I dedicate it to my wife, Tenley Conway, and my son, Thomas Hackworth. I thank Tenley for coming to Canada with me, for sharing her life with me, and for indulging my obsession with American politics. Thomas has been very helpful at teaching me to sing "O Canada" in French and scrambling the Amazon.com algorithm's attempt to come up with books that might interest me with his reading preferences; I am pretty certain that I am the only person whose "recommended books" include pieces by Jerry Falwell, Karl Marx, and Big Bird from Sesame Street.

Faith Based

INTRODUCTION

A Force for Good Greater Than Government

On February 5, 2009, scarcely two weeks after his inauguration, President Barack Obama delivered a short speech announcing that he was continuing one of his predecessor's most controversial programs, the White House Office of Faith-Based and Neighborhood Partnerships, albeit with a slightly altered focus.[1] Given Obama's background as a community organizer in Chicago — one that involved a great deal of work with churches (Obama 1995) — it is perhaps unsurprising that the new president decided to retain and improve the office rather than abolish it as some of his supporters had called for him to do. Much more surprising was the language he used in his speech. While carefully highlighting the compassion that motivates many faith-based organization (FBO) volunteers, and the positive works of FBOs in general, the president inserted a conspicuous phrase that was picked up and repeated by wire services as the embodiment of what he is trying achieve with the office: "No matter how much money we invest or how sensibly we design our policies, the change that Americans are looking for will not come from government alone. There is a force for good greater than government" (White House Office of the Press Secretary 2009). "A force for good greater than government" became the next day's headline in many newspapers. Whether he intended it or not (and if one reads the full speech, it is apparent that his point was much subtler than this), the president had repeated and reinforced the notion that the work of faith-based organizations is more virtuous, or at least more capable, than that of government-sponsored welfare.

It is easy to overemphasize casual phrases buried within much larger speeches — to take things out of context and assign meaning later — but Obama's invocation of this notion is a seductive point of departure for a variety of more substantive contextual reasons. Above all, Obama had just won an election by repudiating his predecessor's antigovernment policies. The Faith-Based Initiative was one of President George W. Bush's most controversial programs.

With two wars and an economy in shambles on his plate, it is intriguing that Obama decided to foreground such an issue so early in his administration. Why did he do this? Was it a simple case of political pandering? Possibly — Obama did make inroads with the evangelical Christian community during the election, and perhaps this was an attempt to nurture those votes. But it is also possible that Obama's casual invocation of the benefits of faith-based institutions marked something more significant, namely, the discursive normalization of faith-based organizations as a suitable replacement for government-provided welfare. It is possible that the president was simply repeating a widely held assumption among the electorate — that government-based welfare is manifestly inferior to faith-based care — even if his own views on the topic are considerably more complex.

This book explores the political mobilization of this sentiment — individualistic, antigovernment, but proreligious notions of welfare — over the past thirty-five years in the United States. In short, this book is about "religious neoliberalism" — its theological origins, its political orientation, and its power to motivate mainstream policy and ideas. It is not intended to impugn or second-guess those who are motivated by faith to provide aid to the poor. The critical angle is directed at the *idea* of deploying that motivation as a justification for eliminating the state's role in welfare or, more generally, in society. To be sure, this topic is often associated with the Republican Party or the Religious Right. It is impossible to ignore the institutions and movements that underlie the religiously conservative Right — nor would I want to — but if Obama's turn of phrase indicates anything, it indicates that this rationality is deeper than the Republican Party or the high-profile ideologues who promote this view as a panacea to solve sundry social ills.

Religious neoliberalism did not originate when George W. Bush was inaugurated in 2001. It did not evaporate when Obama was inaugurated eight years later. It is a sentiment that has great political power precisely because it cuts across a number of different political and theological perspectives. Simply put, many people have political axes to grind with the welfare state, and a great number of people view their form of worship as a suitable means to replace it. But while this sentiment has been mobilized successfully to bond ostensibly different logics, it contains the seeds of its own destruction. Although religious neoliberalism may have a great deal of political value as a casually held notion, it has been and continues to be a divisive force when discussions of implementation begin. And these divisions are not just between Right and Left, promarket and antimarket, but rather extend to an important division within the Right itself. Religious neoliberalism, in short, poses an irresolvable ideational problem for both neoliberalism and religious faith — one that apparently led to the unraveling of arguably the most powerful, if unlikely, political coalitions of the past thirty years in the United States.

The central thesis of this project is that religious neoliberalism is an ideational fragment held by a variety of ostensibly different groups — religious conservatives, neoliberals, religious social welfare activists, and the like. It is thus an ostensibly seductive platform — in abstract terms — to bond groups that seem to be fundamentally compatible. The rationality of replacing secular welfare with religiously delivered welfare has helped to bond together elements of the American Right throughout the past thirty-five years.

It has bonded neoliberals motivated by hatred of government intervention in economy and society with religious conservatives motivated by a desire to foreground religion in public life. But it has also served in a more mainstream sense to soften the hard-edged language of neoliberal social policy. Demolishing public housing, cutting social security, eliminating food stamps, and cutting Aid to Families with Dependent Children (AFDC) all sound harsher than relying on the compassion of churches to serve the poor. It is a sentimentality that moderates neoliberalism and fuels antistatist, antiwelfare antipathy. But because it is ultimately an internally contradictory conception, it actually functions to widen gaps not only between fragments on the Right but between Right and Left. This book is an exploration of this process.

PLAN OF THE BOOK

There is a great deal of theoretical ground to cover before a book of this sort can be properly situated, so chapter 1 examines the foundations of religious neoliberalism and how it has been considered by other scholars. By and large the exercise reveals that this sentiment is more a political ideal than a policy reality; few if any faith-based organizations have successfully replaced a meaningful segment of the welfare state even in symbolic form. Some on the Right suggest that this is because government welfare "crowds out" charities (Richards 2009); those on the Left suggest that it is because faith-based organizations — diffuse and disparate as they are — do not possess the capacity to ever meaningfully replace the welfare state. Either way, it is clear that religious neoliberalism is an idea, first and foremost. Chapters 2 through 4 explore the deployment of this idea at three levels — first, as it is promoted theologically; second, as it is debated among evangelicals; and third, as it appears in mainstream public dialogue. But while it is evident that no ideal-type instances of a completely independent religious welfare sector exist to study, some types of welfare are venerated more than others, and there are recent instances of policy makers attempting to inch closer to such a reality. Chapters 5 and 6 consider two such experiments: gospel rescue missions and efforts to rely on religious charities following Hurricane Katrina in 2005. Above all, these experiments reveal that idealized replacements for the welfare state are, at best, rare, if not completely nonexistent — the state is still centrally involved in both. But they also illuminate a political truth that serves as the focus for the remainder of the book, namely, that religiously inspired welfare and neoliberalism are two different projects that may have made convenient bedfellows but that create more tensions than their promoters would like to acknowledge, revealing more fissures than anything else. This opening of fissures has been a useful reminder of the partiality of both processes — one that can enhance our understanding of many other sociopolitical movements.

CHAPTER ONE

Faith, Welfare, and Neoliberalism

TAX DAY TEA PARTY, 2010

The lead-up to the event was impressive, well funded, and stoked the curiosity of those across the political spectrum. Freedom Works—the generously funded conservative advocacy group—had engineered and mobilized a year's worth of rage against health-care reform, "big government," and regulation. Tax Day was meant to be not only the culmination of its efforts but an opportunity to unveil its "Contract from America," a thinly veiled takeoff of the early 1990s "Contract with America," which was credited with returning Republicans to congressional power in 1994. The new contract, like the old one, was filled with boilerplate conservative positions on deregulation, lowering taxes, fighting crime, and maintaining a pugnacious posture abroad. Freedom Works and the conservative intelligentsia promised a rally on Tax Day that would number in the tens of thousands, maybe even exceed one hundred thousand. But when April 15 finally arrived, the turnout was disappointingly small, no more than four thousand on the spacious National Mall. What the event lacked in numbers, it made up for in diversity of ideology, on the Right, that is. Though the participants were almost entirely white, the ideological variation expressed through the many placards and signs was an intriguing window onto the multifarious motivations among members of the Right in the United States.[1]

There were signs that seemed singularly focused on government debt ("your kids are China debt slaves"), those that focused on gun laws ("I'll keep my guns, freedom, and money . . . you keep the change"), on abortion ("abortion sucks, abort our 44th prez"), the welfare state ("I am an enemy of the welfare state"), and many advocating the perception that the United States was slipping into despotic socialism ("hey Obama, we refuse to trade our Constitution for your Marxist agenda"). There were signs that were meant to personally diminish the president as a person—racist parodies of the president, the president in white face, the president's face imposed on Stalin's — and of course there were signs that expressed simple rage at the "leftist establishment." In perhaps the most concise expression of this sort, a white Ford pickup truck circled the rally with the expression "angry mob on board" streaked across its tinted windows. These signs were the focus of media attention, of Facebook parodies, of discussion by cable news pundits. "Rage against out-of-control government" was the prime talking point that emerged from the mainstream analysis.

But there were also other fragments of the conservative movement represented on April 15. They received comparatively less press but are of particular interest for this book. First, there were dozens of signs expressing affinity for the work of Ayn Rand. "Who is John Galt?" "Where is John Galt?" and "Please forward this doctor's mail to Galt's Gulch" — all references to Rand's *Atlas Shrugged*, in which the rich, tired of being taxed and regulated, leave society to form a colony in Galt's Gulch — were but a few examples of the references to Rand. Second, dozens of signs referenced the Bible in some way. Most were issue oriented — references to the immorality of abortion or gay marriage or to the importance of defending Israel. Others were more general and ominous; one sign simply quoted Hosea 4:6, reading, "Because you have ignored the law of your God" (beneath this verse was a picture of a ship labeled "America" sinking into the sea). Some of these signs tried to fuse biblical morality with libertarian ideals. One sign quoted Proverbs 16:26, "He who labors, labors for himself," followed by the editorial addition, "not the state" (figure 1.1). These signs — those that attempted to fuse the individualistic, antistatist, procapitalist politics of the Right to Bible-is-inerrant fundamentalism — are particularly curious in the context of both the Tax Day rally and the recent history of the American Right.

On the one hand, such a fused sentiment is not so surprising. Ayn Rand has always been a sort of folk hero on the American Right for her strong anticommunist stance, pro-individualist politics, and relatively successful efforts to create a conservative cultural counterbalance to Hollywood and the publishing industry. Her books, *The Fountainhead* (1943) and *Atlas Shrugged* (1957) — both later adapted into films — were popular during their time and have remained so among conservatives for venerating the individual, markets, and an antipathy for government. Moreover, the Religious Right has been a strong supporter of small government, promarket politics in the United States throughout the past thirty years. Jerry Falwell's *Listen, America!* (1980), a call for conservative evangelicals to reassert themselves in American politics, is an argument for reorganizing the economy and society not just according to scripture but also

Tax Day tea party, 2010, Washington, D.C.

along the lines of Milton Friedman. Marvin Olasky's equally influential *Tragedy of American Compassion* (1992) is similarly a mixture of promarket neoliberalism and scripture. In this diatribe against the secular welfare state (and paean to the church-based welfare of the eighteenth and nineteenth centuries), Olasky acknowledges (and liberally cites) both God and Milton Friedman as key inspirations. So on the one hand, finding religiously conservative activists with placards celebrating a different kind of conservatism (neoliberalism) is not terribly surprising. But on the other, a more serious reading of either the history of neoliberalism or the evangelical Right in the United States exposes the complexity of this conflation.

The veneration of Ayn Rand is particularly curious and instructive. Rand was a publicly avowed atheist. Many of her religiously conservative contemporaries hated her not only for this position but also for her insistence that Christianity (like all religions) was not to be trusted, because its ethics of cooperation contradicted the principles of individualism. Rand once deemed Christianity "the kindergarten of socialism" on these grounds (Burns 2009). Similarly, while it is possible to find among the Religious Right ideologues like

Falwell and Olasky who have venerated the free market and vilified regulation, one can also find many counterexamples of religion being used to motivate a socialist politics. In short, the invocation of the Bible to justify neoliberalism is a highly contested practice. By the same token, however, it is difficult to deny the role that the merging — or fusion — of religious conservatism and neoliberalism has played in the political promotion of the American Right. Ever since the public effort in the 1960s to put aside differences for the purpose of electoral success, neoliberals (those primarily interested in deregulation, lower taxes, and individual-first public policy) and religious conservatives (those whose primary political inspiration is a relatively literal reading of the Bible) have not only supported each other but have used their own ideology to justify the other (Sager 2006). Neoliberals have venerated religion in general and religiously oriented charities as suitable alternatives to the state, following the ideas of thinkers like Milton Friedman and Friedrich Hayek. Religious conservatives have used biblical verses to suggest a divine justification for cutting taxes, welfare, and regulation. Though their perspectives may originate in separate ideational places, religious conservatives and neoliberals were able to put aside their differences enough to formulate impressive electoral success from 1980 to 2006.

The Tax Day tea party may not have harkened a new dawn of conservative politics, as its Freedom Works overlords had wished, but the event offered an opportunity to open the curtain on conservative politics as they existed in 2010. It revealed that the Right, despite its organizing successes of the past thirty years, is composed of fragments — movements, ideals, individuals — that have organized around electoral success but originate in and are destined for different locales (literal and political). This book is about the political and theological effort to fuse neoliberal politics and religiously conservative politics — the importance this union has represented for the Right; the ways in which the idea has manifested itself; and the influence it has had on actualized policy.

THE NEOLIBERAL TURN

There is arguably no other concept in the social sciences, particularly geography, political science, and sociology, that has garnered as much attention as neoliberalism in the past ten years. It is difficult to summarize the vast literature on this subject, but it includes a variety of attempts to comprehend the rise and growth of neoliberalism — loosely defined as an ideological sanctification of private property, the individual, and antistatist politics. Researchers have documented the rise of neoliberalism as an ideal (Hackworth 2007; Harvey 2005) and the various policy pathways that it adopts in different locales (Brenner and Theodore 2002; Peck and Tickell 2002). Geography has been an active contributor to this literature (though by no means the only field from which this work has emanated) in large part because there is a marked spatiality to the adoption, diffusion, and growth of neoliberalism worldwide (D. Wilson 2004; Mitchell 2004). Put simply, the interaction between local conditions and events, on the one hand, and various attempts by governments, think tanks, and ideologues to impose neoliberalism from above, on the other hand, have created an incredibly complicated and uneven landscape of policy forms (Peck 2006a; Brenner and Theodore 2002). One policy outcome that has been discussed at length is the devolution of welfare from provision by the centralized Keynesian state to nonprofit intermediaries (Trudeau 2008; Katz 2008; Hackworth 2003; Hackworth and Moriah 2006). According to neoliberal thought, charities were "crowded out" by the rise of the welfare state and would grow again to overcome their capacity constraints and represent an improved replacement if government were to reduce its profile or remove itself entirely from the sector (Gruber and Hungerman 2007; Hungerman 2005; Steinberg 1991). The government has, in short, failed according to neoliberals.

The importance of government failures

The idea of government failure is crucial to the narrative of neoliberalism — an entire literature has formed to defend and promote the idea. The "government failure" literature was, and continues to be, built on the political desire to provide an antidote to the notion of market failures that dominated economic thought and policy during the postwar period in the United States and much of the developed world (Liu 2007; Wallis and Dollery 2002; Montgomery and Bean 1999). Market failure economists, especially following Paul Samuelson (1954), focused on ways of using government to reduce inefficiencies and inequities in the production and distribution of goods and services. Though some prominent neoliberals (Hayek 1944, 1960; Friedman 1962) were actively challenging the focus on market failures and explicitly addressing the failures of government during the mid-twentieth century (the apex of the market failures literature), it was not until the late 1970s that a formalized "government failures" literature began to emerge and gain traction. The literature on "government failure" is broad and varied and lacks the theoretical foundation of market failure theory (Liu 2007), but it can be traced to a number of traditions, including the work of Adam Smith (Reisman 1998), Charles Wolf's model of nonmarket failures (Wallis and Dollery 2002), and rational-choice approach, particularly its public-choice "capture" and Austrian political-economy variants (Harris 2007). Whatever the specific source of inspiration, the literature is unified around the desire to develop a concept of "government failure" that is theoretically analogous to market failure.

The actual focus of applied studies within the "government failure" literature is somewhat varied but almost always consists of a case study (or studies) that situates or highlights a public good whose distribution or production was either "corrupted," "distorted," or "inhibited" by the actions of government at some level. To name but a few of the more ambitious examples, Edwyna Harris (2007) argues that misguided regulatory schemes in Victoria, Australia, led to an increase in in-stream salinity, while Clifford Winston (2000) suggests that "government failure" is to blame for nothing less than nearly all public-transit and road-congestion problems in the United States and the United Kingdom. Other articles highlight examples of "public goods" that are successfully produced and delivered by private entities, such as Michael Montgomery and Richard Bean's (1999) study of privately built climate-controlled walkways in North American cities. The latter approach is less common because, as many "government failure" theorists are quick to argue, very few public goods are completely private in their production and distribution (so there are not many examples to celebrate).

In any case, the nature of the "failure" varies somewhat depending on the topic, but the most common "failures" found in the literature are (1) the failure of government to efficiently provide public goods (see Chang 1997); (2) the presence of special interests who have "captured" elements of the government and influence government officials to govern in a nonoptimal way (Wallis and Dollery 2002); and (3) the graft, corruption, and misguided or malevolent intentions of public officials that distort markets (Meier 1993). Most articles that highlight "government failure" end by arguing that privatization is the "answer" to the putative problem. It is unclear the extent to which such ideas are the cause of or simply the product of larger shifts within the broader public sphere (Wallis and Dollery 2002) — as Ha-Joon Chang (1997) argues, they are probably both. At a minimum, as Joseph Wallis and Brian Dollery (2002) point out, the notion of "government failure" has been associated with various efforts in the United States, the United Kingdom, Canada, and New Zealand (among many other nations) to "reform" government — to make it run more efficiently, "like a business" (Box 1999). It is also clear that such ideas have served as an important justification for reducing regulation in the developed and less-developed world alike.

The secular economic bent to this narrative

The prevailing narrative of neoliberalism has foregrounded the importance of secular economics scholars, concepts, and justifications for its rise. The work of economists Friedrich Hayek, Milton Friedman, and Ludwig von Mises are particularly central to this narrative (Peck 2008; Hackworth 2007; Harvey 2005). Though once dismissed as the "lunatic fringe" by a leading historian of liberalism as recently as the 1960s (Girvetz 1963), the ideas of these scholars have become canonical to contemporary neoliberalism. All were engaged in the project of selectively highlighting the ideas of classical liberals — Smith, Hume, Acton, Locke, and (James) Mill in particular. Hayek, Friedman, and von Mises venerated various economic rationalities in the construction and functioning of society, in particular the market, private property, individual freedom, and state deregulation. Along with dozens of like-minded economists, the three formed the Mont Pelerin Society to develop such ideas and advocate their diffusion (Peck 2008; Goonewardena 2003). The ideational influence of scholarly economic thought of this sort on the narrative of neoliberalism is difficult to overstate.

The simple fact that many of its proponents happen to be economists is not the only way in which economic thought dominates the narrative of neoliberalism's rise. A variety of other scholars have highlighted the importance of economic rationalities for this trajectory. Dumenil and Levy (2004), for example, have foregrounded the role of tax policy in this narrative. They argue that neoliberalism may have complicated ideational roots, but its political salience is rooted in a widespread desire among elites to reduce their tax burden (see also Harvey 2005). Other scholars have highlighted the importance of economic logics used by various institutions to promulgate neoliberalism. The logic of neoliberalism is shielded by an ostensibly nonpolitical economics and used to justify "necessary" interventions by global bond-rating agencies like Moody's (Hackworth 2002), global institutions like the International Monetary Fund (IMF) (Peet 2003), and think tanks like the CATO Institute (Peck 2006b). The interventions of these institutions are shrouded in economistic fatalisms: choose the neoliberal path or else . . . your economy will fail; . . . your state will fail; . . . your freedoms will be curtailed.

In general, the role of secular economics — as a set of ideas, as a discipline, as a justification — is central to the growing scholarly narrative tracing the rise of neoliberalism. To be sure, there are good reasons for such a focus. First and foremost, the revival of classical liberalism in the twentieth century was spearheaded largely by secular-minded economists. Hayek, Friedman, von Mises, and their infamous Mont Pelerin Society of like-minded economists became incredibly effective activists for their cause. Second, powerful organizations like the IMF and the World Trade Organization (WTO) are organized around secular economic logics. And third, regardless of whether economic thinking can explain the rise of neoliberalism, troubling material changes to the economy in a variety of locations around the world have been exploited successfully by neoliberalism's proponents. Whether it be the "shock therapy" of mid-1990s Russian economic reconstruction, the stagflation of the 1970s in the United Kingdom and the United States (Harvey 2005), or more immediate "crises" like Hurricane Katrina (Peck 2006a) or the war in Iraq (Klein 2007), secular economic ideas have been used to sell, depoliticize, and promote the growth of neoliberalism.

But while there are certainly valid reasons for using a secular economic lens to understand neoliberalism's rise as an ideology, such an approach falls considerably short of explaining why the idea has political salience. Although we can usefully trace the ideational rise of neoliberalism through economic texts, concepts, and institutions, such an approach does not reveal much about why the idea has gained political traction — why it has been adopted in many different countries, and why it is so appealing during times of crisis when it has such a clear track record of long- and medium-term failure. Some scholars have attempted to deal with this question by widening the scope of ideas beyond those that economists have foregrounded. Kanishka Goonewardena (2003) and Perry Anderson (2000), for example, highlight the importance of political theorists like Francis Fukuyama, who, while certainly not averse to economistic logics, roots his neoliberalism more in the work of Hegel than that of Adam Smith. Other scholars have chosen to grapple with this question by avoiding the canonical neoliberal economists altogether and focusing on the ideology as an almost-autonomous force — an ideology with local manifestations but without formal guidance by idea makers like think tanks. But while these approaches begin the process of understanding the political roots of neoliberal ideology, they both remain ideational (in different ways), ignoring critical political practicalities. Though they encompass more than purely economic rationales, neither approach explains adequately why neoliberalism has gained political traction among nonideologues.

The goal of this book is to consider the ideational underpinnings leading various radical-right Christian philosophical movements to support neoliberalism (particularly the destruction of the welfare state) and then to speculate on the actualized influence that these movements have on welfare policy. I will argue that if neoliberalism were abstracted as an isolated secular project as laid out by proponents like Hayek and Friedman, it would not enjoy nearly as much popular political success as it has had in the past thirty years. Its record on "solving" economic problems is dismal, and there are no popular movements whose central objective is the promotion of neoliberalism. Neoliberalism's ability to morph into, and adapt to, various movements has allowed it to be coupled with ideas that have their own forms of legitimacy, from which neoliberalism can benefit.

Although this angle has not yet been developed in the literature, several precedents and parallel literatures can be used to guide and justify such a focus. First, in a general sense, the work of Max Weber is perhaps the most important precedent to this approach. Weber famously argued that the Calvinist work ethic — particularly as exercised by Puritan sects — conditioned societies in Europe and the United States to accept the premises of liberal capitalism (Weber 1958, 2004). In particular, he highlighted the importance of the theological concept of a divine "calling" for a particular profession, as well as the inclination to save, work hard, and avoid immediate gratification. These features, he argued, were central to the development of the form of capitalism that originated in nineteenth-century Europe (Germany in particular) and have diffused throughout much of Western Europe and North America today. Kenneth Hudson and Andrea Coukos (2005) apply this logic to the 1996 Welfare Reform Act in the United States, suggesting that the deep-seated assumptions identified by Weber had been reborn in efforts to reform welfare — in particular, the notions of people being deserving and undeserving, and the sanctity of work. In a similar vein, Sigrun Kahl (2005) uses a neo-Weberian approach to suggest that the socioreligious underpinnings of various societies throughout the world can be used to explain a great deal about their welfare systems. The Anglo-American system, he argues, is dominated by an intense individualism, rooted in the Calvinist ethic, that opens a political space for policies like religiously based welfare. Weberian work (and the work of neo-Weberians) not only forms a justification for considering the influence of divinely inspired logics on economic tendencies but also provides clues about the particular role of Calvinist thought as it inflects modern debates about welfare, religion, and economy.

A second group of scholars, namely, historians not necessarily working from a Weberian point of view, have also provided perspectives that can play an important precedent role here. The work of historian Boyd Hilton (1986) stands out in particular. Hilton reminds us that evangelicals were among the most fervent supporters of the original classical liberals in late eighteenth-century England and Scotland. To Hilton, though, it is not that evangelicals were actually liberal in a classical sense, but rather that they saw the brutality of economic conditions faced by the poor as God's punishment for "original sin." So while the details of why the status quo existed were viewed differently — for classical liberal economists, massive poverty was simply a "natural" feature of the market; for evangelicals, it was divine punishment — the policy implications were the same: laissez-faire governance. Gordon Bigelow (2005), in an article for *Harper's Magazine*, finds a similar relationship between nineteenth-century evangelicals and economists. These works are important not only because they draw direct connections between the evangelical community and classical liberalism (the foundation upon which neoliberalism is built), but also because they underscore the point that this union, while politically powerful, is rooted in different logics. Evangelicals and classical liberals have historically agreed on a number of counts, but their purposes are often not the same, and their justifications are often rooted in different goals and perspectives.

A third, more contemporary, group of political economists, whose work is unified more by topic than by a particular school of thought, has attempted more directly to understand the interaction between evangelical Christianity and neoliberalism in the United States, or what William Connolly (2005, 2008) deems the "evangelical-capitalist resonance machine." Connolly argues that this powerful machine has created a political space in which different pathways of revenge against nonbelievers (of neoliberalism and of Christianity) have been woven together. He argues that neoliberals and evangelicals work together in a manner that magnifies the intensity of their political critique. He points, in particular, to the importance of the "end times" prophesies that have been influential among some evangelicals, and how this worldview has merged with a critique of secular government institutions. In this view, such organizations, which "persecuted" the true believers before Armageddon, will be punished. In a similar work, Linda Kintz (1997, 2007) argues that Christian fundamentalist literalism has infused economic discourses in the United States, quelling dissent about economic alternatives. The discourse shifts to "surrendering" to reality rather than conceiving alternatives (see also W. Brown 2006).

In short, although no scholarly work deals with exactly the same question, the contours of the approach chosen here — primarily concerned with the intersections between the economic and the theological — are justified by several different schools of thought and precedent studies. These fragments allow us to conceive of "religious neoliberalism" and its role in fusing together disparate elements of the Right in the United States.

Religious neoliberalism?

Before one can refer to the merger of religious conservatism and neoliberalism as "religious neoliberalism," one must deal with the many complications inherent in conflating or connecting them so comfortably. First, it would be difficult to argue that neoliberalism — in the abstract or in specific forms like tax policy — has been the sole or even central plank within the Religious Right, or that there have been no countervailing voices. To begin with, much of the rise of the Religious Right has been consumed with noneconomic issues like gay marriage and abortion. Abstract concerns about "neoliberalism" are seldom mentioned, and even concrete concerns like those relating to tax policies, welfare, and deregulation generally occur within the context of the aforementioned obsession with abortion and gay marriage. Moreover, a number of leading contemporary and historical figures within the evangelical fold advocate policies that could be interpreted as anti-neoliberal. It is certainly the case, in other words, that neoliberalism is challenged by some within the evangelical fold. But these groups have rarely had sustained political success, certainly not when compared with other organizations and ideologues of the Religious Right (Phillips 2006; Wilcox and Larson 2006). Though the Religious Right is composed of hundreds of groups, many at cross-purposes with one another, the predominant focus of evangelical conservatives in the past thirty years has been on less welfare, less taxes, less regulation, and a greater emphasis on markets and property. Identifying several unsuccessful attempts by evangelical leaders to become more economically progressive does not change this fact.

In a second and related hindrance to the comfortable use of the term "religious neoliberalism," several scholars have attempted recently to dismiss, refute, or challenge the neoliberal bent of the Religious Right by highlighting more-progressive theologies or examples that counter the individualist bent of modern evangelicalism. In perhaps the best-known recent case of this tack, Gary Willis (2006) challenges many of the theological justifications for policies put forth by the Religious Right with more-progressive interpretations. Other scholars have attempted to illustrate how left-leaning religious movements in general, and progressive faith-based organizations (FBOs) in particular, can be mobilized to enact policies that challenge neoliberalism (Beaumont 2008; Beaumont and Dias 2008; Conradson 2008; Jamoul and Wills 2008), encourage union organizing (Sziarto 2008), or more abstractly serve as a basis upon which to build a progressive politics of social justice (Ley 1974; Pacione 1990).

Building on longer traditions such as liberation theology and the social gospel, each of these scholars argues persuasively that religion and FBOs can be mobilized for progressive ends. I agree fully that FBOs have the *potential* to be mobilized toward progressive ends, even to inspire activist critiques of the state, but I disagree with the implication that FBOs or any other civil-society institutions are intrinsically progressive or regressive, or that they could be progressive if only they were inspired by the correct biblical verses. My main argument is that FBOs come with a form of built-in legitimacy that can be mobilized for progressive or regressive ends. It is hard to deny the fact that socially conservative evangelicals have been a key force supporting national policies toward neoliberalism in the United States. It is also hard to deny that intricate biblical justifications have been contrived to naturalize this union (see chapter 2).

Third, even in the face of this evidence, it could be argued that these discourses are nothing more than the "fringe" and do not hold any significant sway in serious policy discussions. This is, in fact, the argument that has been made within the mainstream policy studies community. Steven Rathgeb Smith and Michael R. Sosin (2001), to take but one example, dismiss the relevance of Religious Right leader Marvin Olasky's radical views to the debates on faith-based organizations. Olasky (1992) has advocated an almost wholesale return to eighteenth- and nineteenth-century-style charity-based welfare, using his faith as a justification. Smith and Sosin (and others) dismiss this stance as out of touch with the perspectives of most faith-based organizations. Many faith-based organizations have been around for decades, some more than a century, and most have agendas and organizational structures that are far more varied and far less ideological than Olasky would like them to be. Why would the rise of a few radical Christians really affect this?

To begin with, elements of the Religious Right have influenced such debates with a logic rooted in particular theologies. Though they are certainly extreme, it is difficult to dismiss the importance of biblical logics affecting the worldviews of a community that may include as much as 41 percent of the adult population in the United States and whose members have become much more prominent in the political elite in recent years (Lindsay 2007). Olasky himself was a chief advisor to Governor Bush in Texas and was the chief architect of the latter's now-infamous phrase "compassionate conservatism." Moreover, neoliberal evangelicals like James Dobson and Rod Parsley remain the heads of large, powerful organizations—think tanks, magazines, televised congregations—that reach large numbers of people who share their faith and at least some of their interpretations of the Bible. Though they may not have convinced every person in America or even every evangelical, they hold a disproportionate influence over the political machinery that shapes policies regarding faith and the economy in the United States. It is also true that, whatever their influence, they have become less marginal in the eyes of many evangelicals and are thus more difficult to dismiss as irrelevant.

In short, there are serious reasons to question any narrative that frames the Religious Right and neoliberal Right as being unified in any unproblematic way. Abundant counterexamples and contradictions to such unity have been raised in recent literature. But it is also true that connections exist, and unfortunately these connections are either dismissed (as irrelevant or sufficiently counterbalanced by other perspectives) or simplistically assumed (and therefore largely ignored) by those who incorrectly frame the American Right as a more or less monolithic entity. A brief return to the place of faith in the recent history of the American Right illustrates both the need to study this topic more closely and the conceptual error of assuming that the "Right" is a singular entity.

FUSION, NEOLIBERALISM, THE FAITH-BASED INITIATIVE, AND BEYOND

George W. Bush was neither the first president to campaign on the idea of lowering the wall of separation between religion and the state nor the first to implement policy to further this end. Not only did Al Gore, his opponent in 2000, run on a similar promise to expand government funding to religiously based social service providers, but such organizations were already actively involved in social service delivery at the time.[2] Lutheran Social Services, Catholic Charities, the Salvation Army, the YMCA, and Habitat for Humanity, to name just the largest and most prominent organizations, had received direct and in-kind government aid for social services for decades. Why, then, were Gore and Bush making promises during their contentious electoral battle about removing barriers to the funding of religiously based social services and increasing funding to religious providers? Why, furthermore, was it so controversial, given that such relationships had already existed for so long?

The political issue on the table in 2000 was at once a banal matter of enforcing an existing law and a deeply philosophical issue that galvanized very different factions on the Right while dividing much of the American electorate. The banal matter at hand was simply enforcing provisions in the 1996 Welfare Reform Act that had already lowered existing barriers to the federal government funding of social services provided by religiously based organizations. The act, famous for "ending welfare as we knew it," included an obscure (at the time) passage about the provision of social services by religiously based providers: Charitable Choice. It was the brainchild of a then-little-known Republican senator from Missouri, John Ashcroft, who actively and successfully campaigned to have language included in the act prohibiting discrimination against religiously based social service providers. His efforts were meant to include not just the aforementioned established providers like Lutheran Social Services but also smaller, congregation-based organizations and groups (of whatever size) that refused to separate their social service delivery from their proselytization efforts. It thus became illegal to summarily exclude sectarian organizations from government contracts for social services. Though President Clinton enthusiastically signed the 1996 Welfare Reform Bill to assure his reelection the same year, his administration's support for the Charitable Choice provision remained languid. He and his officials expressed public support for both the provision and the larger issue but clung to the long-standing litmus test of "pervasive sectarianism" in deciding which religious organizations would be excluded from receiving government money.

The notion of pervasive sectarianism was derived initially from the 1948 Supreme Court case *McCollum v. Board of Education* (Black, Koopman, and Ryden 2004). The matter before the court involved a program of religious instruction offered on the grounds of a public school in Champaign, Illinois. Vashti McCollum, mother of James, a student at the school, objected to the program being held there on the grounds that it violated the U.S. Constitution's establishment clause of the First Amendment ("Congress shall make no law respecting an establishment of religion"). The court ruled 8–1 in her favor and in so doing established rigorous criteria for the forms of funding religious activities could receive. One criterion involves the notion of pervasive sectarianism, the idea that an institution or group is so sectarian that a separation of its religious and secular activities would be virtually impossible. This standard emerged in at least a half dozen Supreme Court cases after *McCollum* and in most of these instances formed the basis for limiting or eliminating a program deemed too religious to benefit from public funds. Ashcroft's Charitable Choice amendment was a thinly veiled rebuke to the idea that an organization's pervasive sectarianism made it unworthy of funds, but the Clinton administration nonetheless held a more or less consistent line of upholding the principle while in office.

So, on the one hand, the election year (2000) rhetoric was simply a matter of deciding how to enforce an existing law. Beneath the surface, though, it involved much more. The legal-technical nature of the public debate belied a much more popular (on the Right), much more philosophical struggle to allow religious social service providers to fill in where state institutions had allegedly failed. In broad terms, the debate emerged as an offshoot of the incredible rise of the evangelical Right in the United States since the late 1980s. Throughout the mid-twentieth century, the evangelical movement actually had an ambivalent relationship with electoral politics in the United States (Sider and Knippers 2005; Casanova 1994). The history of the evangelical movement in the United States, and in particular its main public policy arm, the National Association of Evangelicals (NAE), has seen considerable debate about the proper role of the movement in relation to electoral politics (Green 2005). Between 1920 and 1940, movement politics in the form of opposition to teaching evolution dominated, followed by a reign of quiescent politics after larger public opinion turned against such opposition during the Scopes trial.[3] In the early 1940s, especially after the formation of the NAE in 1941, evangelicals began to engage more formally in mainstream politics, especially in the form of adamant opposition to communism or anything that vaguely resembled it. There were still quiescent factions within the movement, however, until the 1970s, when various groups began to gain political power. After the early 1970s, movement and regularized politics were predominant. Opposition to abortion choice and gay rights has been a particularly influential focal point in this transition. The influence of evangelicals began to grow steadily—save for the embarrassing televangelist scandals of the mid-1980s—until the early 1990s, when they had become arguably the most important force on the American Right. The movement, through various institutions like James Dobson's Focus on the Family, the aforementioned National Association of Evangelicals, and Ralph Reed's Christian Coalition, funneled millions of dollars to politicians like John Ashcroft to sponsor legislation such as Charitable Choice (and a great deal more). The passage and (subsequent lack of) enforcement of Charitable Choice was thus much more than a technical quibble about social service funding. It represented a fundamental philosophical disagreement with secular governance, underpinned by an increasingly successful political movement. Though it would be a stretch to suggest that the faith-based movement had a large number of mainstream scholars behind it, there also emerged in the 1990s a group of scholars whose work attempted to carve out a morally and intellectually justifiable space for "faith-based welfare" in the United States.

The neoliberal viewpoint—in favor of eliminating state intrusions "disguised" as compassionate welfare and continuing the pattern of local nonprofit provision rather than government-led provision—was the most established school of thought in this regard. The antistatism inherent in this view has a long history in the United States but had been reenergized during the Reagan years by the growth of nongovernmental social service providers and by the rise of neoliberal think tanks like the CATO Institute (not to mention sympathetic organizations such as the American Enterprise Institute and the Heritage Foundation). The ideas were also promoted by a cadre of economists, political scientists, and business professors around the world. But while the neoliberal camp was the most established, it was also seen as vaguely (if not acutely) mean-spirited when it came to matters involving the poor, and few outside the right wing of the Republican Party subscribed to a puritanically neoliberal perspective. Its application to the realm of social welfare gained little ground among nonideologues until a peculiar school of thought began to merge this premise (neoliberal antistatism) with a paean to the system of religiously based social welfare that existed more prominently in the late eighteenth and nineteenth centuries.

By far the most prominent figure in this regard was Marvin Olasky, at the time a controversial journalism professor at the University of Texas. Olasky's 1992 book, *The Tragedy of American Compassion*, received relatively little attention among the mainstream social policy community but was wildly influential as a more or less intellectual justification for the policies of right-wing politicians like Newt Gingrich and ideologues like William Bennett—both of whom aggressively promoted the book from the start.[4] The promotional endorsements on the book's cover read like a *Who's Who* of the American Right of the 1990s—Gingrich, Charles Murray, Charles Colson. The acknowledgments, which include God and Milton Friedman, situate the work even more clearly. In it, Olasky argues that the "tragedy" of American welfare has long been its inability to distinguish between the "deserving" and the "undeserving" poor. Giving alms to the poor without consideration of whether they deserve it undermines their ability to help themselves, to link with a community, and to find salvation in God. Olasky argues that this problem has existed at least since the late nineteenth century, but that it accelerated considerably after the Great Society welfare programs of the late 1960s. The Great Society plan was, according to Olasky, a great secularizer of welfare, even those forms of welfare that ostensibly came from churches and faith-based institutions. The poor, in his view, need a form of spiritually driven, tough love if they are ever going to rise from their predicament.

Not surprisingly, Olasky's *Tragedy* was either ignored or lambasted by mainstream critics and historians, most notably for cherry-picking historical examples, while completely ignoring others, to venerate an allegedly idyllic time in the eighteenth century when families, not the state, "took care of their own" (Massing 1992). Many scholars saw it as a mean-spirited polemic built on a highly ideological and cursory reading of American history.[5] But while the reception was tepid among academics, the influence on the American Right was tremendous. Not only was his book promoted aggressively by the aforementioned Charles Murray (famous for arguing that blacks are intrinsically less intelligent than whites), Gingrich (who, as newly elected Speaker of the House in 1994, gave a copy to every incoming first-year Republican congressperson), and William Bennett, but it also caught the eye of a rising Texas politician and businessman named George W. Bush. From the early 1990s onward, the ideas, policies, and strategy of Bush and Olasky would become intertwined. Olasky became an advisor to Bush during his days as Texas governor, his run for the presidency, and eventually his administration.

While Olasky's *Tragedy* had already secured tremendous influence among a group of high-profile right-wing ideologues in the United States, more-serious theologians pointed out the additionally useful fact that the faith-based social service movement in the United States was built on two much older and established European traditions (Daly 2006). Though Olasky's book and ideas were used for more high-profile political debates, the German Catholic notion of "subsidiarity" and the Dutch Calvinist model of "sphere sovereignty" were used to persuade more narrowly focused audiences.[6] Bush, his main advisor, Karl Rove, and even Olasky himself were known to invoke these two principles when speaking to audiences of religious folk who were not yet persuaded that faith-based welfare was right for the United States. As Lew Daly explains, both principles emerged in the nineteenth century as a reaction to the idea that socialism and social universalism were threatening to undermine the power of the church in social welfare in continental Europe (Daly 2006). "Subsidiarity" is the idea that the state—even the secular state—should provide funding to religiously based social welfare agencies; "sphere sovereignty" is the idea that the state should do so without interfering with the methods of welfare delivery. Though Olasky did not deal with these matters in great depth, and they rarely come up in public debates about the topic, the parallel drawn with "tolerant" European countries helped to morally and intellectually legitimize the position that the ostensibly secular U.S. federal government should actively promote sectarian forms of welfare. It helped extinguish, or at least complicate, the view that such an arrangement might lead to a soft theocracy in the United States and conversely to soften perceptions of the antistatist neoliberal viewpoint as mean spirited.

By the time the race for the presidency in 2000 was under way, the movement (political and intellectual) had gained so much ground that it was almost axiomatic that an appeal to its ideas would have to be made on the campaign trail, regardless of party affiliation. The evangelical movement was no longer ambivalent about participating in electoral politics; rather, it was flexing its muscle aggressively during the campaign. Candidate Gore fashioned a faith-based initiative of his own to tap into this movement, but it was clear that Bush was the preferred candidate. On the campaign trail, Bush, along with his advisor Marvin Olasky and countless other sympathizers, continued to outline a program for lowering the barriers to faith-based welfare.[7] They invoked the language of civil rights, arguing that religious folk, particularly mainstream Christians, had been discriminated against by secular governance for years.

After Bush assumed the presidency in 2000, his new administration made no effort to steer clear of controversial, potentially divisive issues like faith-based welfare. One of the new administration's first tasks was to establish the institutional architecture for implementing faith-based welfare (Kuo 2006). First, it established the White House Office of Faith-Based and Community Initiatives to coordinate efforts, generate promotional material and position papers, organize conferences and workshops, and above all, to placate its evangelical base, which was eager to see action on this front. This was followed by the creation of similar offices in the Departments of Agriculture, Commerce, Education, Health and Human Services, Homeland Security, Housing and Urban Development, Justice, Labor, and Veterans Affairs; the Small Business Administration; and the Agency for International Development. The central goal of these changes was to eliminate "barriers" to faith-based providers who had hitherto been "discriminated against" by the federal government. After establishing the institutional architecture within the White House and the executive branch, the administration issued a series of executive orders and pressured Congress to pass regulatory changes that would lower barriers for religious social service providers and provide tax incentives for charitable giving. Finally, it established the Compassion Capital Fund (CCF) in 2002 to build the capacity of faith-based community organizations that were ill equipped to seek out funding due to small staffs, high turnover, difficulty complying with existing regulations, difficulty applying for funds, or difficulty managing existing projects. The nature of the CCF made it clear that the administration was aiming not to enhance the abilities of established organizations like Catholic Charities but rather to support small, primarily evangelical Christian, often congregation-based organizations (many of which would have been rejected for aid by the Clinton administration because of pervasive sectarianism).

The results and aftermath of the Faith-Based Initiative are explored in greater detail later in the book, but it is worth stating here that not only was the Office of Faith-Based and Community Initiatives critical in giving the Bush administration a political identity, it also helped fuse (briefly) elements of the Right—an institutional reincarnation of the attempts at fusion in the 1960s. The ironic twist, also considered later in this chapter, is that the initiative contained the seeds of its own destruction. Ultimately, it has served more to divide the constituencies and logics that it was meant to reconcile. Neoliberals grew frustrated that their issues were overshadowed and downright offended by moralistic interventions like the Terry Schiavo affair in 2005 (Sager 2006). The general public began to question the practicality and compassion in "compassionate conservatism" after Hurricane Katrina. The religious-neoliberal coalition seemed frayed to say the very least, and the national elections of 2006 and 2008 were seen as, in part, a rebuke of this peculiar fusion of interests.

Evidence of endurance of this coalition since 2008 has been mixed. On the one hand, the Obama administration was elected on a much more interventionist, much less (religiously) moralistic platform that relied very little on the votes of either neoliberals or religious conservatives. Within a year of gaining office, the administration embarked on a number of initiatives that alienated both religious conservatives and neoliberals: resumption of stem-cell research; a massive stimulus bill; the assumption of ownership of several banks and two large car manufacturers. But on the other hand, the administration has not abandoned the faith-based program outright and has even expressed mild support for some of its most controversial provisions.[8] Moreover, the coalition itself shows signs of reformulating in various incarnations of the Tea Party movement—arguably the most significant opposition to the Obama administration. Initially Tea Party activists tended to be more secular, but a late 2010 poll showed signs of a merger between the two factions. Among self-identified religious conservatives, 69 percent reported support for the Tea Party, and as of early 2011 religious conservatives were the most rapidly growing group within the movement (Pew Forum 2011). The electoral success was impressive—the Tea Party energy was key in the 2010 congressional elections for the Republicans. But there are still signs of tension as some Tea Party leaders have publicly rebuked the entry of religious conservatives to "their" movement (Koelkebeck 2010). As of 2011, it was not at all clear where the coalition was headed. But it is clear that the tenuous connection between religious conservatives and neoliberals continues in some form. Whether it is a marriage of electoral convenience (as it appeared to be in 2010) or something more ideationally organized (with think tanks and prominent ideologues trying to make links like those outlined in chapter 2) remains to be seen.

FAITH-BASED ORGANIZATIONS AS REPLACEMENTS FOR (FAILED) GOVERNMENT WELFARE

One singularly beneficial outcome of the Faith-Based Initiative was the scholarly attention that it generated. From this literature, it is clear that the notion of faith-based organizations is far from uncontroversial. Despite the fantasy of those at the CATO Institute, very few FBOs see themselves, or are seen by others, as literal replacements for government-run welfare. Some, in fact, see themselves as promoters of more welfare and expanded regulation. It is useful to examine this literature to illuminate the variety of conceptions related to FBOs.

There has been a great deal of effort in the past decade to provide a better typological understanding of FBOs, particularly in relation to how and when religion is a part of the social services they provide (Hula, Jackson-Elmoore, and Reese 2007; Reingold, Pirog, and Brady 2007; Kearns, Park, and Yankowski 2005; Jeavons 2003; Hiemstra 2002; Twombly 2002; Smith and Sosin 2001). The literature reveals that FBOs are positioned and understood in at least four ways: as extensions, enhancements, catalysts, and alternatives (both regressive and progressive) to government-based welfare. These themes are both idealized archetypes revealed in discourses and actualized practices in which FBOs are engaged. The purpose, method, and audience vary radically among the studies present in the literature, but they provide considerable insight into the relationship between FBOs and state-based welfare. Much of the literature allows ample room for hybridity; most studies emphasize a great deal of complexity within and between FBOs, thwarting simplistic attempts to essentialize them. By the same token, many FBOs are organized around, and characterized by, themes that are more coherent than an opinion survey of their volunteers might imply, and regardless of the level of hybridity, it is valuable to create conceptual reference points, drawn from the existing literature, to structure this study.

FBOs as extensions

A common theme in the literature on faith-based organizations is the revelation that many FBOs engage in social assistance financed by some level of government. Usually, though not always, such contractual work is performed by large denominational groups (rather than congregations) like Catholic Charities and Lutheran Social Services. Almost all federal-level and most state-level contractual agreements in the United States (and most secular, developed countries for that matter) include guidelines on how the money can be used. Often these include stipulations requiring the FBO to guarantee that it will not discriminate against those of other faiths in hiring or clientele. In order to comply in such cases, intricate efforts have been made either to secularize the operation or to compartmentalize and separate a branch of the organization that will deal with government contracts (from the "sectarian" branches of the organization that might not comply with government regulations). This tends to diminish the openly religious elements of FBOs, much to the consternation of conservatives who believe that these elements are integral to organizational success (Hackworth 2010b). In a sense, then, some FBOs — or at least components of some FBOs — function as extensions of state-based welfare, committed in general to the same principles of universal access as secular government and largely dependent on the state for funding. They are, in this view, part of the "shadow state" that has become increasingly relevant as central governments spin off welfare work in the form of contracts to nongovernmental organizations (NGOs) (Trudeau 2008; Staeheli, Kodras, and Flint 1997).

FBOs as enhancements

Not all literature emphasizes the contractual "shadow-state" functions of some FBOs. Some authors emphasize the notion that FBOs may depend on government funding because of their fundraising limitations (Briggs 2004) but are better than the state at providing social services and so should be given the latitude to use this funding however they wish, sectarian or not. This theme reveals itself in a number of forms. First, one school of thought in the literature emphasizes the role that FBOs have played historically as social service providers before and during the rise of formalized government-funded welfare and argues that their efforts merit government funding. This position argues, based on a historical perspective, that FBOs have displayed compassion, accumulated social capital, and enhanced community in ways that government or secular NGO welfare could not hope to achieve. Authors in this school conclude that this historical experience is a justification for contemporary funding of FBOs, with no (or few) regulatory strings attached. This theme was popular within the Bush administration, which tried, with mixed success, to increase funding to and reduce oversight of small congregational FBOs (Kuo 2006; Black, Koopman, and Ryden 2004; Dilulio 2004).

A second manifestation of the FBO-as-enhancement theme has been in the form of geographical accounts of how the relationship between FBOs and the state functions in countries other than the United States. Daly's work is particularly important in this regard, as he argues that Western European countries — particularly the Netherlands and Germany — offer a model in which

FBOs are funded without regulation by the state (Daly 2006). A third argument has been made by conservatives who suggest that FBOs are superior to government-run welfare because FBOs are able to sort the "deserving" from the "undeserving." From this perspective, the FBO as enhancement is not only more just but also less expensive in practice, as the "undeserving" are removed from the care apparatus and the public benefits from better accountability over its tax dollars (Mead 1997, 2003).

FBOs as catalysts for change

Not all authors have understood FBOs as alternatives, extensions, or enhancements of the state. Some have focused on the progressive possibilities of FBOs — how in particular they can be used as vehicles to motivate the state to become more redistributive. Michael Pacione (1990), for example, has documented the importance of the Church of England's *Faith in the City* report of the late 1980s. *Faith in the City* argues for the government to devote more resources to poverty reduction. In a sense, its position is more progressive than that of the official opposition at the time (though probably no more successful). More recently, Justin Beaumont and Candice Dias have argued that the characterization of FBOs as vehicles of neoliberalism is hasty and in many cases inaccurate (Beaumont and Dias 2008; Beaumont 2008). They show how two Dutch FBOs (one in Rotterdam, one in Amsterdam) not only offered conventional social assistance but also provided a vehicle for activism *against* neoliberal policies by the state. Much of this sentiment implicitly (and sometimes explicitly) harkens back to the progressivist ideas of liberation theology and the social gospel — fragments of which have been revived in the form of a "Religious Left" that considers it imperative to use biblical teachings as a justification for challenging the neoliberal state.[9] Still others have pointed out how FBOs have been important components — usually, though not exclusively, in conjunction with labor unions — in advocating for better working conditions and pay for workers (Sziarto 2008).

FBOs as alternatives to the state

FBOs are sometimes framed within the literature as alternatives to the state. It is useful to differentiate the two main forms of this viewpoint because they imply (and in some cases state directly) completely different normative policy agendas. In one case, the experience of FBOs is interpreted as a justification for more state-based or state-sponsored social assistance. In the other, the experience of FBOs is framed as a justification for diminishing or eradicating state involvement in welfare.

Type A: FBOs as alternatives to the regressive state. Some literature focuses on FBOs as alternatives to government systems but not part of a values-oriented desire to destroy state-based welfare. Rather, a number of authors have emphasized the historical and contemporary role that FBOs—congregations in particular—have played in providing assistance that the state either could not or would not provide. First, a variety of authors emphasize the role that FBOs have played historically, specifically before, during, and after the rise of Keynesian welfare in the mid-twentieth century (Cnaan et al. 2006; Cnaan et al. 2002; Cnaan, Boddie, and Wineburg 1999; Wuthnow 2004; Spain 2001). Through case studies and meta-analyses, these authors demonstrate that FBOs have been positioned not necessarily as representing a reason to provide less government welfare but rather as a de facto safety net within contexts where regressive politics has mobilized statecraft to deny social assistance to the poor. They have been an "alternative" because the state would not mobilize its resources to help (Hilfiker 2003).

A second, less direct, strand of thought emphasizes the idea that some FBOs possess qualities that the state simply cannot replicate and thus provide services that are incomparable to those provided by the state. David Ley and R. Allen Hays, for example, have shown how FBOs possess a cultural legitimacy among religious adherents that can motivate volunteers to build houses for the poor or help immigrants assimilate in a new country (Ley 2008; Hays 2002). Though this theme is expressed in varied fragments, the important continuity is that this literature does not support a normative view that would seek the reduction or demolition of welfare. These authors either express the position that FBOs have stepped in where the state has been negligent or, more directly, that FBOs need *more*, not less, help from the state for their social assistance programs.

Type B: FBOs as idealized replacements for the "failed" state. The notion of FBOs as replacements—an idea defined here as encompassing descriptions and practices that frame FBOs as not only better than the state but also capable (or conceivably capable with the right policy) of functioning as independent entities—is less common in the literature, but is voiced by a variety of influential pundits. This theme has taken at least two distinct forms.

First, the idea is rooted in the notion that charities of all sorts, religious or not, were "crowded out" by the expansion of government welfare in the 1930s and remain so today (Richards 2009; Gruber and Hungerman 2007;

Hungerman 2005; Steinberg 1991). According to this logic, the government should radically downsize, if not completely eliminate, welfare so that the charitable sector can be revived (Ziegler 2005). In the words of Jay Richards, an Acton Institute Fellow who released a book in 2009 titled *Money, Greed, and God*,

> Some private charities are more effective than others, but almost all of them are more effective than larger government programs. . . . All of these organizations have one thing in common: they define their mission in part by what the government does or doesn't provide. If the government weren't occupying most of the charitable ecosystem, charities would be profoundly different. The ecosystem would be filled with thousands of well-funded responsive charities accountable to their donors and communities. As it is, government has invaded the ecosystem, and mostly made a mess of it. (Richards 2009, 56)

As a large component of the charitable sector, FBOs are often framed in these narratives, by default, as a suitable replacement for welfare.

Second, this view has been promoted by those who not only dislike government-based welfare but who also believe that the replacement should be religious (not a secular NGO model).[10] Marvin Olasky is arguably the most prominent promoter of this position (Olasky 1992, 2000). He contends that government-based welfare is an abject failure primarily because it is wasteful and does not sufficiently emphasize personal responsibility. In Olasky's opinion, such programs should be dismantled and replaced with locally based, religious systems funded by tithes. Such programs would not burden the federal government, he argues, and would be better able to sort the "deserving" from the "undeserving" poor (Hudson and Coukos 2005; Kahl 2005). As noted previously, Olasky's views have had wide influence in the U.S. Republican Party, much of which stems from his role as advisor to George W. Bush in the 1990s and his creation of the concept of "compassionate conservatism" (Elisha 2008; Harris, Halfpenny, and Rochester 2003; Boleyn-Fitzgerald 1999; Dolgoff 1999).

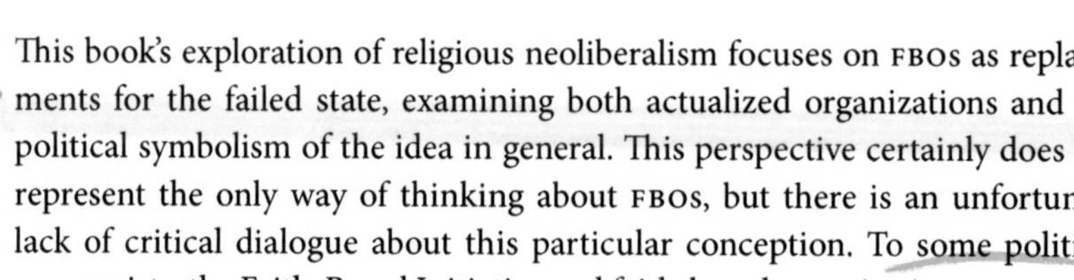

This book's exploration of religious neoliberalism focuses on FBOs as replacements for the failed state, examining both actualized organizations and the political symbolism of the idea in general. This perspective certainly does not represent the only way of thinking about FBOs, but there is an unfortunate lack of critical dialogue about this particular conception. To some political economists, the Faith-Based Initiative and faith-based organizations more generally are an obvious attempt to undermine or downsize the welfare state. But many scholars of FBOs consider this goal of undermining the welfare state to be nothing more than the extremist view of a few who do not reflect the broad landscape of religious organizations involved in welfare. To religious conservatives, the idea of a more sectarianized welfare state is a political ideal — one that motivates a veneration of current work that fits this archetype and energizes a political movement focused on continuing to move the welfare state in that direction. Given the political heat generated by the topic, it is curious that more scholarly work has not been done specifically in this area.

This book is an attempt to open such a critical dialogue. Most assuredly, neither the specific notion of replacing the welfare state with religious providers nor the more general idea of merging theological and secular motivations for neoliberalism is the only way to think of faith, neoliberalism, or welfare, but given the events of the past thirty-five years — in particular the rise of neoliberalism and the Religious Right, accompanied by the ideational dismissal of socialism — it is crucial for students of American politics to consider this question more carefully.

CHAPTER TWO

Religious Neoliberalism(s)

This chapter catalogs the sectarian ideational supports for neoliberalism in the United States during the past thirty years. My argument is that neoliberalism, as an abstract set of ideas, was rarely politically popular enough in its own right to change policies; rather, it benefited from and was legitimated by other discourses and ideas. In a sense, it needed these ideas — mostly borrowed from other corners of the American right wing — to gain political traction. In the United States, various right-wing factions forged an uneasy alliance starting in the 1960s (Sager 2006). The coalition was composed of three broad camps: (1) religious social conservatives who drew much of their inspiration from a literal reading of the Bible; (2) economic conservatives, hereafter "neoliberals," who were drawn to the ideas of laissez-faire; and (3) military conservatives devoted to American intervention abroad (Diamond 1995). Many actualized policies fell into, or originated from, more than one of these camps, making coalition politics possible. For example, policies that increased the tax benefits of donating to religious charities were popular with both social conservatives and neoliberals. Wars fought to open markets to American consumers were popular with both neoliberals and military conservatives. But many actualized policies also strained the coalition. Strong-handed intervention to, say, limit abortions might appeal to social conservatives but not necessarily to neoliberals. Similarly, current antiterrorist efforts to increase surveillance may be popular with military conservatives but are generally not popular with neoliberals. In short, many policy ideas have tested the broad right-wing coalition that has held significant but vacillating sway in American politics for the past forty-five years.

One ideational realm that has traditionally challenged right-wing coalition politics involves the role of the state in economy and welfare. Neoliberals have been, and remain today (despite recent events), steadfastly opposed to almost all forms of state intervention, particularly as they relate to social welfare. Religious conservatives, on the other hand, are a far more complicated group when it comes to this topic. Not only are noted religious leaders of the past and the present open to strong state intervention in welfare, but influential interpretations of the Bible have been used by a variety of scholars and clergy to justify *more* state intervention. For neoliberals and social conservatives to remain allied on the Right, the rhetoric of one camp (or both) would have to soften so that a bridge could be built. This chapter examines one such "bridge" in recent American history: sectarian voices that have emerged in the last forty years to promote economic conservatism in taxes, welfare, and government spending. Not only do these voices teach us much about the tenuous right-wing coalition that introduced and ushered in neoliberal policies in the United States; they offer insights into the ways in which religious ideals can be stretched and adapted for secular political purposes.

NEOLIBERALISM FOR GOD'S SAKE

The following discussion focuses on the politics of conservative Christians, or the Religious Right, largely because of the important role this group has played in the formation of the political Right in the United States (Phillips 2006). This group's perspectives emanate from an overwhelmingly white and Protestant positionality, and it is precisely this orientation that has been deployed to sanctify certain neoliberal principles, so it is useful to review (and to keep in perspective) here. It is also worth noting that despite the superficial uniformity of the origin of these ideas, the Religious Right is actually a highly varied group of people, faiths, congregations, and organizations (Wilcox and Larson 2006). I do not mean to disregard this variation entirely, but the focus here is on illuminating those organizations and ideas within the evangelical fold that maintain the same political goals as neoliberalism. Which evangelical submovements have built-in critiques of the secular interventionist state, welfare, regulation, or taxes? Which, moreover, venerate or sanctify the market and property relations?

Three submovements stand out in this regard. First, Dominionism—the belief that Christians should take control of government and (in its more extreme forms) impose biblical law—provides ample justification for criticizing the secular interventionist state and its institutions. Second, Christian libertarianism, while small in terms of adherents, provides the most direct and comprehensive biblical justification for neoliberalism. Third, prosperity theology provides a biblical justification for embracing the market and property rights. Though rejected by many theologians, its practitioners are highly influential, and its adherents are numerous. These movements are described in the following sketches, which are based on academic and popular accounts of each from both supporters and critics. Four key questions are addressed in each description. First, what is the definition and evolution of the idea? Second, what biblical justification is used to legitimate the idea? Third, how large or influential is the community organized around the idea? And fourth, who are the key promoters and what is their influence? The overall goal is to explore how neoliberalism is promoted and legitimated by these religious logics.

Dominionism

Dominionism, also known as dominion theology, is the largest and most encompassing of the logics considered here, and it is also perhaps the one held most widely as an assumption by evangelicals in the United States. It is also the most internally varied and controversial of the three logics under consideration. As Sara Diamond, a sociologist credited by many with coining the term "Dominionism" explains, "Dominion theology . . . was really more of a world view than a discrete set of tenets. Essentially, Dominionism revolved around the idea that Christians, and Christians alone, are biblically mandated to occupy all secular institutions until Christ returns. By definition, Dominionism precluded coalition or consensus-building between believers and non-believers" (1995, 246). The idea is derived from a controversial interpretation of two passages in Genesis: "And God said, Let us make man in our image, after our likeness: and let them have dominion over the fish of the sea, and over the fowl of the air, and over the cattle, and over all the earth, and over every creeping thing that creepeth upon the earth" (1:26 King James Version); "And God blessed them, and God said unto them, Be fruitful, and multiply, and replenish the earth, and subdue it: and have dominion over the fish of the sea, and over the fowl of the air, and over every living thing that moveth upon the earth" (1:28 KJV). Dominion theologians interpret these passages as an invitation to unabashedly infuse Christian people and principles into secular government, and in the U.S. context, to "return America to its Christian roots."[1] Diamond coined the term, but the belief system itself is often traced to the work of former Dutch prime minister Abraham Kuyper (1837–1920). Kuyper, a Calvinist, asserted that all human actions are part of building God's kingdom. Given that he is generally considered a pluralist, it is ironic that his ideas are now deployed by Dominionists in an attempt to exclude non-Christians from government. Many credit Kuyper today with the concept of state funding for faith-based agencies, and the idea that the mixture of religion and government is not improper for a liberal democratic state (Daly 2006).[2] In the U.S. context, this perspective was co-opted and radicalized most prolifically by two theologians, Francis Schaeffer

(1912–84) and Rousas Rushdoony (1916–2001). Schaeffer's highly influential book *The Christian Manifesto* (1982) calls on Christians to lose their ambivalence about infusing their religion with their politics. According to Schaeffer, it is not only permissible for evangelical Christians to aggressively advocate the Christianization of government, it is their responsibility.

Rushdoony extended and radicalized this notion further by suggesting that theonomy—biblical law—be imposed on the United States. Many consider his work the beginning of an even more extreme version of Dominionism, called Christian Reconstructionism. In this worldview, an extrapolation of Old Testament biblical law would be imposed, including "capital punishment for homosexuality, adultery and abortion; a ban on long-term debt; a return to the gold standard economy; the abolition of income tax; and the destruction of the government welfare system" (Diamond 1989, 240–41). Certainly the most prolific, and arguably the most influential, living Reconstructionist is Gary North.[3] The son-in-law of the late Rushdoony, North was an active member of secular libertarian groups when he was young but became a strict Christian Reconstructionist later in life—so strict in fact that he rejected Rushdoony and Schaeffer as moderates on various issues. North was formally trained as an economist and retains a strict Austrian School libertarian perspective (Clauson 2006).[4] He founded the Institute for Christian Economics, a think tank that produces books and material ridiculing secular government, particularly welfare and government redistribution (Diamond 1995). His books are written in a more popular style and are widely available in Christian bookstores in the United States. Reconstructionists like North invoke an eschatological urgency for this agenda by suggesting that it is the duty of Christians to impose such an order before Christ returns to earth. Their belief system is "postmillennial" in that they believe Christ's followers will have to rule the earth for one thousand years before his return; thus it is urgent for Christians to take over and replace secular government now. This position contrasts with that of "premillennialists," who believe that Christ will return before this time to usher in the one thousand years of Christian rule, so it is less urgent to institute political change immediately. In either case, Reconstructionism is widely viewed by both followers and critics as the most extreme form of dominion theology.

As a label, Dominionism is highly controversial. Above all, it was coined by a sociologist who is widely critical of the American conservative movement, Sara Diamond (1989, 1995, 1998) and repeated frequently by a religion scholar who has made a career of criticizing the Religious Right, Frederick Clarkson (1994). As such, some conservative journalists, writers, and leaders have dismissed the label; one author has called it "conspiratorial nonsense" (Kurtz 2005), and another has referred to it as an attempt "to smear the Republican Party as the party of domestic theocracy" (Williams 2005). Others who are less defensive point to the fact that figures like Rushdoony and ideas like Reconstructionism are not shared in a wide doctrinaire way by evangelical Christians. Still others note that most conservative evangelicals are premillennialists in orientation and thus are not predisposed toward demonstrating the urgency of postmillennial Reconstructionists. But regardless of the label followers choose, it holds true that the foundational ideas of Dominionism — or whatever we choose to call it — are important to many evangelicals (Rudin 2006).

The Religious Right, for example, has made the appointment of sympathetic judges a key agenda item over the past thirty years in part because of Dominionist assumptions. Moreover, the idea that Christians should hold dominion over the earth has been mobilized recently to motivate more-moderate politics, as reflected in the pro-environmental stance of an increasing number of evangelicals (Cizik 2005). Thus, as William Martin (1996) and others suggest, the label is more hotly contested than the idea itself.[5] As Martin points out in reference to an interview he did for his book *With God on Our Side*,

> Because it is so genuinely radical, most leaders of the Religious Right are careful to distance themselves from it. At the same time, it clearly holds some appeal for many of them. One undoubtedly spoke for others when he confessed, "Though we hide their books under the bed, we read them just the same." In addition, several key leaders have acknowledged an intellectual debt to the theonomists. Jerry Falwell and D. James Kennedy have endorsed Reconstructionist books. Rushdoony has appeared on Kennedy's television program and the 700 Club several times. Pat Robertson makes frequent use of dominion language; his book, *The Secret Kingdom*, has often been cited for its theonomy elements; and pluralists were made uncomfortable when, during his presidential campaign, he said he "would only bring Christians and Jews into the government. . . ." He added, "There are a lot of us floating around in Christian leadership — James Kennedy is one of them — who don't go all the way with the theonomy thing, but who want to rebuild America based on the Bible." (1996, 354)

Dominionism may not be its followers' label of choice, but it encapsulates a belief system that is less disputed than its label.

In part because of the discomfort the label inflicts on many followers, it is difficult to arrive at solid figures on the size of the "Dominionist community." Rushdoony once estimated the number of Reconstructionists at twenty million (Sugg 2005), but he gave little reason for arriving at this figure, so it is difficult to tell how accurate it is. More relevant, perhaps, is the fact that the writings of

Dominionists and Reconstructionists are widely available, and many Religious Right figures have expressed public sympathies for the ideas or used them as justification for various political interventions. Diamond expresses this well:

> What is important about Reconstructionism and other expressions of dominion theology was not so much the eccentricities of its key advocates but rather that diffuse influence that America was ordained as a Christian nation and that Christians, exclusively, were to rule and reign. Most activists in the Christian Right were not well versed in the arcane teachings of Rousas Rushdoony [and other Reconstructionist ideologues]. . . . But there was a wide following for softer forms of Dominionism. Among the most popular of Christian Right ministries was one called WallBuilders, a lucrative book and tape sales operation, that promoted the claims that America's Founding Fathers were nearly all evangelical Christians, and that the only answer to rampant social problems was for Christians alone to run for elected office. (1995, 248)

The work of North and others was also useful for creating a vague system for many of the arguments that have emerged in the United States over the past several decades regarding welfare, taxes, and the state in general. The ideas have become less radical as more and more adherents express their support. Dominionist ideas have been voiced in recent mainstream discussions of topics ranging from environmentalism to economics to faith-based welfare.

So what influence does Dominionist thinking have on the adoption of neoliberalism in the United States? First and foremost, Dominionism is a foundational assumption held by many evangelicals. It creates a theological justification for opposing various forms of government intervention, whether through protest against "activist" judges or the promotion of political figures who will "return America to its Christian roots." Second, Dominionist theology is rooted to a neo-Calvinist perspective that is both antistatist (when it comes to welfare) and highly individualistic (when it comes to poverty). Thus, Dominionism helps deepen and sanctify the critique of secular welfare. Yet by the same token, Dominionist theology is a shaky foundation upon which to build neoliberal politics, so we should not overestimate its influence. In particular, Dominionism, while opening a space for criticizing secular government, envisions a top-down theocratic state that would certainly not appeal to purist secular neoliberals like Hayek. Similar to Boyd Hilton's (1986) description of the alliance between economic liberals and evangelicals in eighteenth-century England and Scotland, modern-day neoliberals and Dominionists may share a common enemy, but their endgame is considerably different. In politics, though, the antipathy toward secular interventionism has been shared strongly enough by Dominionists and neoliberals to consider their relationship — while shaky and headed for different ends — a powerful alliance of convenience.

Christian libertarianism

Christian libertarianism is a loosely organized effort to synthesize the often-juxtaposed projects of conservative Christianity and secular libertarianism. It is a hybrid movement that does not draw on a single line of scholars, theologians, or ideologues, but because many of the latter — both contemporary and historical — are powerful adherents who edit national magazines, write for journals, and run think tanks, it is worth considering the influence of this particular construction. The most frequently cited biblical verse in support of this position is John 8:36: "If the Son therefore shall make you free, ye shall be free indeed" (KJV). Beyond this, Christian libertarians have drawn on three principle sources of inspiration for their movement. First, Christian libertarians have turned to classical liberals who integrated some degree of Christianity into their liberal writings, the two most famous being John Locke and Lord Acton. Acton (1988) was the most outspoken in this regard and now has a think tank named after him. In one of his more frequently quoted passages, he sets out the synergy between his Christianity and his liberalism: "Liberty is not the power of doing what we like, but the right of being able to do what we ought. . . . Liberty is the prevention of control by others. This requires self-control and, therefore, religious and spiritual influences. . . . [In Western countries] Liberty has not subsisted outside of Christianity."[6] Second, and related to this synthesis, Murray Rothbard (2006) outlines the three "libertarian experiments" by early American colonists in North Carolina, Rhode Island, and Pennsylvania. He suggests that the libertarianism of these early colonists was heavily influenced by and infused with Christian principles. Third, a number of others, including Harro Höpfl (1991), have gone back much further to suggest that the Lutheran Reformation was based on a form of Christian libertarianism. Höpfl argues that "libertarian, egalitarian, communal motifs were part of the texture of his [Luther's] theology" (xii). Whatever the source, the basic premise of Christian libertarianism is that society should aim for the maximum feasible freedom within a biblical framework, primarily that of the Ten Commandments.

There is, however, a great deal of controversy concerning this notion, arising from both secular and sectarian corners. Some "libertarian Christians," who are quick to argue that they are not the same as "Christian libertarians," quibble with the latter's interpretation of biblical verses and the notion that lawmakers should intervene with moral "crimes" that have no obvious victim, such as lust. Christian libertarians believe that such crimes should be punished by the state, while libertarian Christians believe that government should exist only to punish crimes that victimize other people (Olree 2006; Antle 2007). Other theological differences between Christian libertarianism and libertarian Christianity include the former being more likely to be tied to theonomic or Reconstructionist views. Overall, though, both camps draw inspiration from the aforementioned verse (John 8:36) and are deeply skeptical of the interventionist secular state, particularly in its manifestations in the form of taxes and social welfare.

Most secular critics, however, either do not make such a nuanced theological distinction or are focused on a deeper contradiction that they see within Christian libertarianism, namely, that libertarianism is an intrinsically secular ideal involving a small state. It is thus incompatible to call oneself a "libertarian" if one considers "biblical sins" like abortion, adultery, or homosexuality, or vices like alcohol, gambling, and prostitution to be punishable by the state. Ryan Sager, for example, is deeply skeptical about the sustainability of the alliance between libertarians and Christians that undergirds the Republican Party in the United States. He notes that there has been an effort to "fuse" the two perspectives since the 1960s, but it has always been a tenuous alliance: "Whatever alliances have been formed, libertarians have always tended to see social conservatives as rubes ready to thump nonbelievers on the head with the Bible the first chance they get, and social conservatives have always tended to see libertarians as dope-smoking devil worshippers" (2006, 8). Despite these differences, Sager explains that "these two warring factions would ally to take over the Republican Party. By 2004, forty years later, they would dominate the entire country" (2006, 21). But to Sager, this alliance of convenience, albeit powerful, is beginning to break apart the Republican Party (see also Kirkpatrick 2007). He envisions secular libertarianism and evangelicalism as fundamentally incompatible. Others have expressed skepticism about the potential longevity of a tightly fused alliance but have nonetheless identified ground for overlap. Doug Bandow (1994), for example, shares some of Sager's skepticism but goes much further in trying to build bridges between Christianity and libertarianism. While Bandow doubts that the connections are as firm as some argue, he does see ample ground for overlap:

> Even Christians who are not libertarians and libertarians who are not Christians have many opportunities to cooperate on protecting religious freedom, restricting state expansion, encouraging private education, keeping the government out of child care, opposing welfare systems that destroy families, and so on. And

> given both groups' need to find additional allies, it is increasingly important that Christians and libertarians not only talk with each other, but work together. (1994, 34–35)

The areas Bandow identifies reveal what such an agenda might look like in an actualized political sense.

Others have attempted to steer clear of the basic philosophical compatibility issues between libertarians and Christians by simply renaming the movement but still accepting its basic premises. Michael Lienesch, for example, deems Christian libertarians "Christian capitalists" and explains that

> in constructing their economic thinking, they borrow heavily from secular conservative writings, which they cite and combine in a seemingly unsystematic way. The writers they refer to most frequently include libertarians of the Austrian school of Frederick A. Hayek and Ludwig von Mises. . . . Among the currents that come together to form this theory of Christian capitalism, libertarianism seems to run the deepest and strongest. Religious conservatives turn easily to free market economic theory, and they draw heavily on the Austrian school thinkers such as von Mises, Hayek, and Murray Rothbard. In a free market theory they find the fundamental principles of their economic psychology, including individual self-interest, the profit motive, and free enterprise. Borrowing from these themes, Christian capitalist thinkers translate their meanings, turning free market theory, with its free-wheeling and forward-looking emphasis on entrepreneurship, into a more restrained and more pessimistic theory of self-discipline and social order. (1993, 107–8)

Still others have tried to turn the debate to a consideration of the aforementioned historical roots of the movement to legitimate it and downplay its internal contradictions. Murray Rothbard (1980, 2006), for example, though not a self-identified "Christian libertarian," has suggested that an individual's religion should not preclude his or her ability to be a libertarian.[7] He acknowledges that many present libertarians are atheists but emphasizes the fact that historically many libertarians have been Christian:

> There is no necessary connection between being for or against libertarianism and one's position on religion. It is true that many if not most libertarians at the present time are atheists, but this correlates with the fact that most intellectuals, of most political persuasions, are atheists as well. There are many libertarians who are theists, Jewish or Christian. Among the classical liberal forebears of modern libertarianism in a more religious age there were a myriad of Christians: from

> John Lilburne, Roger Williams, Anne Hutchinson, and John Locke in the seventeenth century, down to Cobden and Bright, Frederic Bastiat and the French laissez-faire liberals, and the great Lord Acton. (Rothbard 1980, 11)

In short, considerable theological and secular controversy has surrounded the Christian-libertarian alliance, but it would be misleading to say that this has undermined its importance for a powerful group of adherents.

Although as W. James Antle (2007) laments, Christian libertarianism is "at a disadvantage without a theological tradition robust enough to compete with the Social Gospel on the left or Christian Reconstructionism on the extreme right," it nonetheless has some very powerful advocates. Arguably the most powerful individual currently pushing a hybrid agenda of Christianity and libertarianism is and was Marvin Olasky. As described earlier, Olasky was a journalism professor at the University of Texas during the late 1980s and early 1990s; he is currently editor in chief of the widely read *World Magazine*. As author of over two hundred articles and books, frequent talk-show guest, advisor to President George W. Bush, and popular journalist, Olasky has directly woven libertarianism and conservative Christianity into public policy discussions (Grann 1999). Prior to the 1990s, Olasky was a relatively obscure professor, but this changed dramatically with the publication of his infamous book *The Tragedy of American Compassion* and then the rise of governor then president George W. Bush. *Tragedy* is a harsh critique of the secular welfare state. It venerates the religious charity-based approach of the eighteenth and nineteenth centuries, which was able, Olasky argues, to separate the "deserving" from the "undeserving" poor, and which drew on community resources, rather than those of the federal government. The book was welcomed with open arms by the rising Republican congressional delegation, whose leader Newt Gingrich famously delivered a copy to each freshman congressman in 1994. Olasky's neo-Calvinist "tough-love" approach to poverty softened the political edge of antiwelfarism (and antistatism) intrinsic to libertarianism (and to the Republican Party platform at the time) (Grann 1999). It also helped build a platform that would bring George W. Bush to power. Olasky was a direct advisor to Bush in Texas during his gubernatorial campaigns and is credited with devising the language of "compassionate conservatism" (Olasky 2000). While Olasky has not inspired a theological movement and does not have a literal congregation, his connections to powerful people and his mainstream credentials give him and his ideas legitimacy never achieved by extremists like North and Rushdoony.

Related to this mainstream legitimacy, the ideas of Christian libertarianism are also promulgated by the Acton Institute for the Study of Religion and Liberty, named for the aforementioned patriarch of the movement, Lord Acton. The Acton Institute was founded in 1990 in Grand Rapids, Michigan, and is directed by Robert Sirico (Acton Institute 2008). The aforementioned Marvin Olasky and Doug Bandow are board members, among others. Through its journal (*Journal of Markets and Morality*), its magazine (*Religion and Liberty*), and its newsletter (*Acton Notes*), the organization promotes a blend of libertarianism and Christianity. Much like Olasky's focus, the Acton Institute aims not to devise or build a particular theological movement but rather to promote the hybrid perspective of libertarianism and Christianity in public policy discussions. Though less powerful than some secular libertarian think tanks like the CATO Institute, it is recognized as influential, certainly the most influential proponent of its particular perspective.

Christian libertarianism and related variants make up the smallest "movement" discussed in this chapter. But by the same token, the Christian libertarian idea is promoted by people and institutions more powerful than either Dominionists or prosperity theologians. Moreover, it is the most direct attempt to weave together neoliberalism (otherwise known as libertarianism) and conservative Christian theologies. It creates a biblically justified forum for critiquing secular government, particularly taxes and welfare. It tends to be less extreme than Reconstructionism but for the most part shares the view that the Bible creates parameters that some secular libertarians are unwilling to accept. So, as with Dominionism, Christian libertarianism shares an intellectual enemy with neoliberalism but has a very different ideal endgame. It creates a theological justification for abhorring big government, taxes, and welfare, and has had a great deal of behind-the-scenes sway in recent public policy discussions in the United States.

Prosperity theology

Prosperity theology—also known as Prosperity Lite, Health and Wealth, Word of Faith—is a controversial movement built around the idea that God wants people to be prosperous and that it is their duty to donate heavily to their churches in order to activate this outcome. It is most often associated with the charismatic and Pentecostal wings of Christianity. The basic philosophy is preached in three of the four largest churches in the United States: Joel Osteen's Lakewood Church in Houston, T. D. Jakes's Potter's House in Dallas, and Creflo Dollar's World Changers Church near Atlanta. Historians, theologians, and critics differ somewhat on the historical origins of prosperity theology, but three viewpoints are cited most commonly. Randy Alcorn argues that traces of the movement can be found as far back as the ancient Pharisees, who "lived and breathed Prosperity Theology and relished labeling everyone beneath their social caste as 'sinners'" (1989, 104). Robert Jackson (1989), by contrast, traces modern-day prosperity theology to the mid-twentieth-century metaphysical cults popularized by Kenneth Hagin and Essex Kenyon. Hagin and Kenyon were popular Pentecostals in Texas and Oklahoma who sponsored revivals, radio shows, and newsletters in the 1940s and 1950s. And finally, the most commonly cited origin for modern prosperity theology (and the one that creates the most controversy for the idea) is the series of 1980s televangelist movements that were led by now-disgraced preachers Jimmy Swaggart and Jim Bakker.

A variety of biblical verses are used to justify the position that God wants his followers to be prosperous, but those cited most often are the following:

> DEUTERONOMY 8:18 (KJV): But thou shalt remember the LORD thy God: for it is he that giveth thee power to get wealth, that he may establish his covenant which he sware unto thy fathers, as it is this day.
>
> MALACHI 3:10 (KJV): Bring ye all the tithes into the storehouse, that there may be meat in mine house, and prove me now herewith, saith the LORD of hosts, if I will not open you the windows of heaven, and pour you out a blessing, that there shall not be room enough to receive it.
>
> JOHN 10:10 (KJV): The thief cometh not, but for to steal, and to kill, and to destroy: I am come that they might have life, and that they might have it more abundantly.

Each is used by prosperity theologians to promote the view that authentic piety toward God will be rewarded with material wealth. This serves, whether by design or by default, as a salve for the guilt of wealth experienced by many Christians and as biblical justification for little or no focus on the goal of poverty amelioration that dominates other theological schools within Christianity, particularly liberation theology and the social gospel.

There are, of course, many critics of this interpretation of the Bible and the political and cultural attitude it is believed to foster. Secularists have repudiated the idea as essentially an offshoot of disgraced 1980s televangelist schemes that demanded heavy financial contributions from parishioners and brought great riches (and eventually public shame) only to its leaders.[8] But it is also seen as simply supporting, with biblical legitimization, the immediate gratification, greed, and self-interest already rife in American society (Wolfe 2003). As Alcorn elaborates,

> In Prosperity Theology, God is seen as a great no-lose lottery in the sky, a cosmic slot machine in which you put in a coin and pull the lever, then stick out your hat and catch the winnings while your "casino buddies" (in this case, fellow Christians) whoop and holler (or say "Amen") and wait their turn in line. . . . In this sort of system, God's only reason for existing is to give us what we want. If we had no needs, God would probably just disappear—after all, what purpose would he have anymore? With this kind of slick (and sick) theology, prayer ceases to be sacred. Instead of a means to give him glory and draw strength for the battle, prayer degenerates into an endless "wishlist" to take before our Santa God. (1989, 116–17)

Finally, some regard prosperity theology as little more than a form of pandering by religious entrepreneurs aiming to build their congregations by promoting a vision toward which parishioners will gravitate. As Shayne Lee (2007) notes,

> It is ironic that Pentecostalism, the branch of Christendom that once harbored ardent anti-secular sentiment, transformed into a new Pentecostal movement with the strongest embrace of technology, secularism, capitalism, and popular culture. . . . These ministries emphasize the therapeutic benefits of the faith and offer an optimistic view of the future that embraces American ideals of prosperity. In our competitive religious landscape, churches that adjust to cultural changes are flourishing while traditional churches lag behind and lose many members.

In general, there are a variety of secular criticisms of prosperity theology. Some consider it a view that promotes greed, justifies inequality, and at worst leads to fraud cloaked in religion. But while secular critics abound, many religious scholars too have expressed deep misgivings about the philosophy.

There are several theological critiques of prosperity theology, but they can be grouped broadly under the argument that its preachers base their message only loosely on the Bible, and that their views are contradicted more often than supported by scripture. Rick Warren, pastor of the famous Saddleback Church in California, is a key critic of the prosperity theology movement. "The idea that God wants everyone to be wealthy?" he commented skeptically, explaining, "There is a word for that: baloney. It's creating a false idol. You don't measure your self-worth by your net worth. I can show you millions of faithful followers of Christ who live in poverty. Why isn't everyone in the church a millionaire?" (quoted in Van Biema and Chu 2006). And Warren, though probably the prosperity movement's most famous theological critic, is not alone. Theological scholars have contested the use and interpretation of the aforementioned biblical verses that underlie the movement. As Jackson, just one of many examples, argues, "To preach a Christian lifestyle that must involve perfect health, enough wealth to live off the fat of the land, and the ability to call, at whim, upon God to interfere with history on one's behalf, is to preach a faith that has no true biblical precedent. Prosperity theology is therefore heretical because its claim to be Christian cannot be substantiated, and the faith movement is to be rebuked wherever it is encountered" (1989, 22–23). Preachers like Warren and scholars like Jackson point to numerous other biblical verses that contradict prosperity theology's emphasis on material wealth. Three verses are cited most commonly in this regard:

> 1 TIMOTHY 6:10 (KJV): For the love of money is the root of all evil: which while some coveted after, they have erred from the faith, and pierced themselves through with many sorrows.
>
> MARK 10:21 (KJV): Then Jesus beholding him loved him, and said unto him, One thing thou lackest: go thy way, sell whatsoever thou hast, and give to the poor, and thou shalt have treasure in heaven: and come, take up the cross, and follow me.
>
> LUKE 18:22–25 (KJV): Now when Jesus heard these things, he said unto him, Yet lackest thou one thing: sell all that thou hast, and distribute unto the poor, and thou shalt have treasure in heaven: and come, follow me. And when he heard this, he was very sorrowful: for he was very rich. And when Jesus saw that he was very sorrowful, he said, How hardly shall they that have riches enter into the kingdom of God! For it is easier for a camel to go through a needle's eye, than for a rich man to enter into the kingdom of God.

Theological critics point primarily to these and other verses to reinforce their position that prosperity theology is at best loosely supported, and at worst blatantly contradicted, by the Bible. But while the movement has been harshly criticized by secular and religious scholars, it is hard to escape the fact that it is very influential in some parts of the country; its promoters reach millions of people per week through televised sermons that construct a biblical justification for wealth accumulation.

As with all religious movements, it is difficult to obtain firm figures on the number of adherents to prosperity theology, not least because it is both a formal theological movement with members who self-identify as such and a set of assumptions that are likely more widespread. Alcorn (1989) says simply that "millions" adhere to the philosophy in the United States but does not specify further. *Time* magazine (Van Biema and Chu 2006) teases us with the estimation that prosperity theology "has been percolating in the 10 million–strong Pentecostal wing of Christianity" and goes on to argue that many of its assumptions are even more widespread, but this is the limit of the magazine's specificity. In the same article, the authors report on a poll commissioned by their magazine showing that while only 17 percent of Christians self-identified with the prosperity movement, 61 percent felt that "God wanted them to be prosperous," and 31 percent felt that "if you give your money to God, God will bless you with more money." So while the formal adoption of prosperity is somewhat limited, its central assumptions appear to be widely held by evangelical Christians in the United States.

But while the number of formal adherents is certainly important, the direct and indirect reach of several of prosperity theology's more high-profile proponents suggests that the movement may be broader than simple congregational surveys suggest. The movement is led by many of America's most influential preachers, and many others integrate key elements into their ministries. Joel Osteen is one of the most controversial of these figures and arguably prosperity theology's most ardent supporter. Osteen pastors Lakewood Church in Houston, Texas.[9] He succeeded his father, John Osteen, to its pastorship in 1999 and has since built the ministry into one of the largest in the United States, with over 40,000 congregants (Van Biema and Chu 2006). He also reaches approximately 2 million people in 150 countries through his weekly television broadcasts (Lakewood Church 2008) and is a best-selling author, most notably of *Your Best Life Now: 7 Steps to Living at Your Full Potential* (2004) and *Become a Better You: 7 Keys to Improving Your Life Every Day* (2007), both of which have topped the *New York Times* best-seller list (Contemporary Authors Online 2008a). In his books, broadcasts, and sermons, Osteen preaches an optimistic self-help message that is, by his own admission, less deeply rooted in scripture than that of some other ministries (Van Biema and Chu 2006). Other famous prosperity ministers include T. D. Jakes and Kirbyjon Caldwell. Jakes is also a prolific best-selling author and a prominent figure in the African American community (Pappu 2006). His ministry preaches much more than just prosperity theology, but he is unapologetic about the association, seeing it as an optimistic interpretation of the Bible that empowers his congregants. In addition to weekly sermons at his 30,000-person Potter's House Pentecostal Church in Dallas, Jakes is a frequent talk-show guest and travels widely for speeches, including one he delivered in the Georgia Dome, where he reportedly broke the attendance record with over 84,000 people (Contemporary Authors Online 2008b; Winner 1999). Caldwell, though presiding over a "mere" 15,000 parishioners, is more noteworthy for his personal connections as President George W. Bush's pastor at the United Methodist Church in Houston, Texas. He gave the benediction for Bush's first inauguration and recently presided over the marriage of Jenna Bush. Caldwell preaches a moderated form of prosperity theology.

Prosperity theology certainly has its critics, but it would be difficult to argue that it is a "fringe movement" given the influence of figures like Osteen, Caldwell, and Jakes. But it is more than a formal theological movement. It is also a set of biblically legitimated assumptions, and these assumptions reinforce some of secular neoliberalism's main objectives. First, prosperity theology provides divine justification for what many are able to justify otherwise only in crass capitalist terms: accumulating wealth. It softens, contradicts, and muddies the notion that accumulation is the disreputable pursuit that socialists and progressive theologians cast it as. Second, it reinforces the Calvinist tenet of individual responsibility for material success, and its darker corollary, individual responsibility for one's failures—a key justification for dissolving the welfare state. Third, prosperity theology sanctifies private property as an expression of piety. It provides a rationale not only for focusing on one's own wealth creation—separate from community or society in general—but also for ignoring the poverty of others. If "God wants you to be rich," as a recent *Time* magazine article impishly pondered, then it is not too much of a stretch to assume that being poor is a form of justified punishment.

FINDING NEOLIBERALISM IN RELIGIOUS LOGICS

The rise of neoliberalism over the past several decades has been traced by a variety of geographers, sociologists, and political economists. Though the foci of these accounts vary considerably, a central theme is the importance of both economic thought and material conditions in the rise of the ideology. Neoliberalism, in this account, is the brainchild of Hayek, Friedman, and von Mises, who revived and promoted the works of the classical liberals in the Mont Pelerin Society and via interventions throughout the world. It caught on for material reasons, namely, the fact that 1970s stagflation undermined the rationale for Keynesianism and (more cynically) the wealthy wanted lower taxes. I certainly do not seek to diminish this narrative. Not only have I helped author it; I also still believe it to be largely correct. But what I do question is the ability of this script to assist in understanding the *political* diffusion of the neoliberal ideal despite neoliberalism's failure to achieve its putative ends and solve the problems it was situated to address. Surely, neoliberalism has benefited from ideational links with other political movements that have their own built-in legitimating rationales. This chapter has explored the importance of one such complementary framework of thought: evangelical logics that support neoliberalism, even if indirectly or accidentally.

While neoliberalism is primarily a secular economic creation, it has benefited politically from the prominent rise of the evangelical movement in the United States. This is not to say that every corner of the evangelical movement supports neoliberalism or that we can automatically assume that evangelical Christianity would lead to the same supportive outcome in other countries. The trajectory of neoliberalism in the United States is based on a convergence of three religious logics that has created intricate faith-based rationales for supporting neoliberalism's main tenets, which emphasize individual responsibility, deregulation, low taxes, and antiwelfarism in particular. All three of these influential religious logics are deeply, though not exclusively, influenced by neo-Calvinism, and as such they share as much as they differ, yet each is aligned with a particular set of institutions, tactics, and theologies worthy of separate consideration. Though they each face both secular and sectarian critics, all these movements lend credibility to neoliberalism by reinforcing its agenda. Dominionism invokes divine inspiration for challenging the secular state. Christian libertarianism cites divine justification for abhorring socialism and the welfare state. Prosperity theology deploys divine absolution for accumulating capital. Each draws inspiration from the Bible and, as such, invokes a legitimacy rooted in faith. They are influential for different reasons. Though formalized Christian Reconstructionism is most assuredly a fringe movement, the basic assumption of its ideational colleague, Dominionism, saturates the politics of the Religious Right, and conservatives in general. Christian libertarianism does not have an intricate theological justification, but it has well-connected promoters who have influenced recent policy. And prosperity theology, though derided by many theologians as a heretical mirage, is the organizing principle for some of the most powerful, widely heard preachers in the United States.

It would be a stretch to suggest that these are the only ideas percolating on the religious or neoliberal Right in the United States. It would also be misleading to imply that these ideas are uncontested within or outside the evangelical fold. I am categorically not making this argument. But by the same token, it is difficult to avoid the curious parallel rise of neoliberalism and fundamentalist religious movements, and the role they have collectively played in bonding and promoting the Republican Party. Religious ideas — even of the fragmentary and extremist variety — are an important and understudied component of this picture. But they remain only part of the picture. The following chapter grounds these ideas by exploring the more pedestrian and less ideological views of moderate evangelicals on matters pertaining to the state, welfare, and taxes.

CHAPTER THREE

Compassionate Neoliberalism?

One particularly useful contribution to the literature on neoliberalism (made by geographers primarily) has been the notion that while it is valuable to understand the relatively global formations of an idea — emanating from think tanks, high-level politicians, and meta-organizations like the IMF — the actual adoption and diffusion of ideas and policies are far more contingent, locally and institutionally (Brenner and Theodore 2002; Hackworth 2007). Put simply, although it is crucial and often challenging to understand the machinations of the think tanks, ideologues, and politicians who promote an idea, the actual adoption or formation of that idea is filtered and influenced by a variety of influential forces at a variety of scales. Religious neoliberalism may be an idea that Gary North, the Acton Institute, and the Republican Party frequently promote, but these are hardly the only, or even the most important, influences on those who adopt, reject, or accept part or all of its assumptions. To grasp the ways that such puritanical ideas (religious neoliberalism) are filtered by other forms of legitimacy at a variety of scales, we can benefit from observing how the idea is processed and communicated by those who are not explicitly trying to promote it. This chapter explores ways in which the "evangelical community" has communicated and processed ideas related to welfare, government, and taxes.

While it is true that the evangelical community is a crucial element in the political rise of religious neoliberalism, many commentators have carefully avoided essentializing an "evangelical stance" on a variety of issues because the evangelical community is so internally varied. As Clyde Wilcox and Carin Larson (2006), among many others, observe, the range of people who self-identify (historically and in the present) as evangelicals is vast, and not all evangelicals align with the Right generally or the specific institutions of the Religious Right. There is also incredible ideational variation within both the Religious Right and the wider evangelical community on many issues. Some of this variation is regional (southern evangelicals versus northeastern evangelicals), some of it demographic (white evangelicals versus black evangelicals), and some generational (views of young evangelicals versus older evangelicals on gay marriage). In short, evangelicals and the Religious Right are both more varied than they are popularly portrayed.

The topic of social welfare is both particularly salient to this chapter and a vivid illustration of this point. As Omri Elisha (2008) among others illustrates, a tension exists within the evangelical community around the concept of government-funded welfare. On the one hand, it is a central part of evangelical identity to care for those in need—which is often an important ethical component of supporting social welfare. On the other hand, the political identity of the majority of evangelicals aligns with the conservative movement—a tenet of which is the partial, if not complete, dismantlement of government-funded welfare. Thus, while evangelicals tend to vote for political figures who advocate the reduction or elimination of welfare, most evangelicals have fairly complicated views on the topic that tap into this core conflict between anti-statism and compassion. This chapter excavates and analyzes evangelical positions on welfare as a vehicle for speculating about the role such positions may play in both complicating evangelical political identities and influencing public policies. The chapter explores the framing of welfare in two evangelical texts—National Association of Evangelicals (NAE) policy resolutions and *Christianity Today*—with these questions in mind. The following sections place particular emphasis on direct and implied positions regarding social welfare and the government's role in welfare provision. I explore several questions, including How are the positions justified, biblically or otherwise? How have these positions morphed into political statements about the "evangelical position"? How has this development affected the erstwhile fusion between neoliberals and evangelicals at the core of religious neoliberalism?

COMPASSIONATE NEOLIBERALISM IN NAE POLICY RESOLUTIONS

The National Association of Evangelicals was founded in 1942 in Saint Louis, Missouri, initially with the name National Association of Evangelicals for United Action (Marsden 1987). The association was formed as an umbrella organization for hitherto disparate denominations and groups. The evangelical community had been reluctant to reenter public policy debates after the Scopes trial in the 1920s, which had the effect of marginalizing evangelicals as antiscience and culturally backward (Green 2005). The formation of the NAE was a crucial first step in the evangelical community's reentry into mainstream politics. The NAE has taken on an increasingly public focus over the years and has assertively entered into various policy debates. As of 2009, the NAE represented over sixty denominations and more than forty-five thousand churches (NAE 2009). The organization is now based in Washington, D.C., and serves to advance evangelical interests in the public policy sphere. One of the many vehicles used to further this agenda is the organization's "public policy resolutions"; they have been used in the past to gauge "the" evangelical position on a variety of issues (Cizik 2005). The resolutions are most often generated by NAE staff but must be voted on by the NAE board during the annual convention. The NAE board, which meets twice per year, is composed of 125 members—50 of whom are denominational representatives, while the remaining 75 fill at-large seats (NAE 2009). The policy issues covered range from immediate responses to policy proposals like the Faith-Based Initiative, to longer-term concerns like opposing communism, to issues that transcend any particular policy initiative, such as abortion, AIDS, and safeguarding the traditional family.[1] The resolutions range in size from as brief as one hundred words to over five thousand words.[2] Overall, each resolution attempts to summarize and promote a stance held by evangelicals on a particular issue. This process is always complicated and often acrimonious, reflecting differences among the variety of constituencies and organizations under the NAE umbrella. There are 219 resolutions in total to date, some of which are publicly accessible on the NAE website, but most of which had to be requested for this book. A total of 41.1 percent of the resolutions respond directly to a particular domestic policy, while 20.1 percent respond to a foreign policy issue during the past fifty years. While all the resolutions involve a moralizing component, some resolutions, 38.8 percent, are not so much specific policy critiques as generalized calls to action, general statements on moral issues, or pronouncements on life in the church.

The topic of government-based welfare for the poor is sprinkled throughout the NAE policy resolutions over the years. The following steps were taken to understand these particular resolutions. First, all the resolutions on every topic were read both to gain a sense of context for those related specifically to welfare and to unearth threads of the discussion about welfare that may not be obvious in the resolution titles. Second, an effort was made to isolate the resolutions most pertinent to the conversation on welfare and its provision by the government. There are no resolutions directly on the topic of "welfare," but dozens that deal with the topic in one way or another. These range from direct responses to policy programs like Charitable Choice, to important references within longer and more general resolutions like "Health of a Nation, 2004" (National Association of Evangelicals Archives 2000, 2004). To maintain focus, some conversations were eliminated from this analysis—such as the many references to private education, communism, and missionary work overseas — even though one could argue that they have some relevance to the issue at hand. Third, resolutions pertaining to welfare were closely scrutinized and the following questions asked: What is the evangelical stance on government-based welfare? What, if any, alternatives are proposed? What themes are most salient in guiding an evangelical public policy on welfare?

Though there is no comprehensive NAE summary of what evangelicals oppose or propose for the welfare state, many definitive fragments can be assembled to reveal the basic contours of "compassionate neoliberalism," at least as it is expressed in NAE resolutions. Overall, a recurrent need is expressed, in some cases framed as a "biblical mandate," to provide for the poor. So while references to welfare in NAE documents may have a generally conservative flair, they do not reflect the "not my problem" libertarianism found in, say, CATO Institute briefings. An evidently genuine concern for the poor is manifested in multiple resolutions (see NAE Archives 1997, 1998). But despite this concern, almost no sympathy is expressed in any of the resolutions for government efforts to address poverty. Almost every reference to welfare includes an implied or direct critique of government-based efforts to solve it. "It is a tragic reality of life in the United States," notes one recent resolution, "that, despite unprecedented economic growth and low unemployment, there remains what appears to be a 'permanent underclass.' This reality persists despite billions of dollars and significant efforts spent on anti-poverty programs" (NAE Archives 1999). Government efforts to eradicate poverty are routinely criticized in the resolutions as inefficient, overly bureaucratic, and leading toward dependency. "We have long maintained," notes one recent example, "that many government programs, while meeting immediate needs, actually weaken families, destroy initiative, and trap people in poverty" (NAE Archives 1997). Small government with a balanced budget is routinely advocated as the alternative (see NAE Archives 1973, 1978a, 1978b, 1984). NAE resolutions outline a system heavily reliant on independent, faith-based organizations, and tax policies that might support them, such as more-generous charitable-giving deduction allowances (see NAE Archives 1964, 1979). Some ambivalence is expressed about the role that government should play in funding such organizations, with opinions ranging from the provision of vouchers to individuals (NAE Archives 1999), to little or no government support (NAE Archives 1979), but there is no ambivalence about the appropriate regulatory role. Regardless of whether it provides funding, the federal government ought to exercise no regulatory oversight of FBO activities, whether in terms of hiring practices, of whom the organization serves, or of how it serves them (NAE Archives 2000, 2004). Not surprisingly, the NAE expresses unambiguous support for the Charitable Choice provision of the 1996 Welfare Reform Act. As a recent resolution states, "The National Association of Evangelicals supports the concept of Charitable Choice, not only as effective public policy, but as a sound expression of faithful Christian discipleship" (NAE Archives 2000). The nature of exactly what this welfare would look like is not covered in great detail in the resolutions, but a recurrent theme is "individual responsibility." As an early resolution states, "One of the fundamental principles of Christian social welfare is to help people help themselves," a concern echoed many times including most recently in 2004 (NAE Archives 1964, 2004).

Within these broad contours, subtler but more definitive messages about welfare are also expressed. These range from comments on where the authority for welfare provision resides, to how evangelicals should understand civil government. These details are expressed repeatedly with conviction and so deserve at least some mention here. First, there are frequent reminders that the Bible, and the Bible alone, provides the clarity needed to craft an evangelical position on welfare. As the 2004 resolution, "For the Health of the Nation," notes, "Every normative vision has some understanding of persons, creation, history, justice, life, family, and peace. As Christians committed to the full authority of Scripture, our normative vision must flow from the Bible and from the moral order that God has embedded in his creation" (NAE Archives 2004). Almost every resolution, regardless of topic, includes the invocation of a biblical verse to justify the stance. This is, of course, not surprising for an organization whose identity is built at least in part on a strict, if not literal, reading of the Bible. But perhaps more instructive about this observation is the fact that there is no apparent evidence of the variation, and indeed dissent, within evangelical ranks about what the Bible calls them to do about various policy realms. Rather, as one resolution points out, the effort is to present a unified voice and to mask such variation: "Evangelicals may not always agree about policy, but we realize that we have many callings and commitments in common" (NAE Archives 2004).

A second theme expressed in the NAE resolutions is a profound discomfort with or distrust of the secular state. Government at all levels is routinely described as possessing almost limitless power and relatively nefarious intent or, at best, well-intentioned incompetence. Most resolutions that deal with the topic cautiously call for government support for FBOs but also frame the state as a corrupting omnipresence that will pollute the evangelical message. Recent and past governmental rules that limit resources to FBOs because of their sectarian bent, or that attach rules to the outlay of resources, are routinely criticized. FBOs are framed as a source of virtue, and government-based welfare as a polluted or misguided project. A corollary to this theme is the unambiguous rejection of the notion that FBOs, particularly evangelical FBOs, serve simply as extensions of the government when they enter into welfare contracts with it. As one representative resolution puts it:

> The church may as an agent administer government assistance without compromise of the principle of the separation of church and state if the church's policies are not controlled or influenced thereby or vice versa. This may be done in conjunction with the church's own relief program or as a separate operation. In consideration of the contractual arrangement between the church and government, certain policies may be stipulated and agreed upon, but the choice of the personnel and total administration of the program must be the entire responsibility of the church. *The church cannot become the arm of the government.* (NAE Archives 1964, emphasis added)

The state is thus represented as a complicated entity within NAE resolutions. On the one hand, there is a begrudging acknowledgment that government has a different purpose than the church and, importantly, has a resource base that could be mobilized for FBOs. On the other hand, the state is routinely cast as a polluting influence. A simple contracting, "extension of government" relationship is definitively and repeatedly rejected. FBO as enhancement is the most common model found in the NAE resolutions.

A third theme prevalent in NAE resolutions about welfare is the frequent invocation of biblical mandates and authority not just for Christians but also for governmental officials and government in general. "Be it resolved," notes a resolution in 1980, "that the National Association of Evangelicals urges Christians to pray for those in authority, and to remind them that their power is ordained of [God] and they are responsible to Him" (NAE Archives 1980). "We affirm," states another, "that government is a God-ordained entity, responsible for the advancement of good and the inhibition of evil in our world" (NAE Archives 1978a). It is not surprising, again given the identity of evangelicals, that biblical verses are invoked as a source of credibility for Christians. But resolutions extend this legitimacy to the entire government. This is interesting not least because it sheds some doubt on the narrative that evangelical welfare is mainstream politically or at least so varied that it is impossible to label. These invocations of biblical authority could easily be deemed "Dominionist" in character. It is perhaps for this reason that one recent resolution softened this point somewhat by more carefully delineating a role for government that is separate from that of the church: "There are scriptural warrants for the instituting of civil government and for the ordaining of the Church, that each has its distinct sphere of operation" (NAE Archives 2003). By and large, however, this sentiment is overshadowed by the many references to biblical authority over government, no matter who is in charge or what welfare program is being administered. This is one of many similar subcurrents also found in the pages of *Christianity Today*.

COMPASSIONATE NEOLIBERALISM IN *CHRISTIANITY TODAY*

Christianity Today is one of the most widely read evangelical magazines in the United States, boasting a circulation of 140,000 and a readership of 290,000 (*Christianity Today* 2009).[3] The magazine was founded in October 1956 by Billy Graham in an attempt to bring together the various denominational and congregational elements of evangelical Christianity (Noll 2006). Graham wanted to create a "theologically conservative but socially liberal" forum to compete with the highly successful *Christian Century*, a mainline Protestant publication popular in the 1950s (Smith 1998). Today's *Christianity Today* is available online and in print. The magazine features a variety of material ranging from op-eds to short articles and longer pieces. Current events dictate much of the subject matter, but unlike in the pages of its secular counterparts, the writers often link the news to biblical verses and themes. Unlike the NAE policy resolutions, *Christianity Today* is not in the business of unifying the evangelical community around short, coherent statements. Also unlike the NAE resolutions, *Christianity Today* articles are highly example-based, offering a rich template from which to generalize about normative ideals for welfare provision. The articles report on the breadth of the community, so there is considerable variation in viewpoints expressed and in how they are justified. That said, *Christianity Today* is generally considered politically moderate compared to other evangelical magazines and periodicals. It is precisely for this mainstream quality that it was chosen over other possibilities for examination here.

A variety of articles from *Christianity Today* were analyzed, including those that feature the words "welfare," "charitable choice," "social assistance," and/or "faith-based initiative."[4] Articles with references to "government," "taxes," "poverty," "regulation," and/or "economic policy" were also included but thinned considerably to retain a focus on social assistance. The *Christianity Today* database, which dates to the beginning of the publication in 1956, yielded 373 articles after the initial sorting process. Each of these articles was then read for content, and a coding scheme was developed to help understand the way that government-based welfare was framed and how, if at all, evangelical alternatives were positioned. Generally, the intent was to count and analyze the articles to address the following questions. First, how are governmental welfare efforts characterized? Are they routinely portrayed pejoratively, positively, or ambivalently? What words are frequently used to describe them? Second, an effort was made to analyze the specific examples of "welfare" that are featured. Of the 373 initial articles on the topic, 92 feature a description of an evangelical NGO involved in social assistance work or abstractly refer to an idealized relationship between FBOs and the state. Special attention was paid to these articles, and two specific questions examined. First, how are evangelical alternatives positioned in these articles? Second, how do these framings compare to the typological family of religious NGOs discussed in chapter 1?

Overall, articles on welfare are sporadic, often appearing around seminal events like the 1960s Great Society programs, welfare reform in the 1990s, or Hurricane Katrina in 2005. There is a great deal of variation in tone, style, length, and substance. Some articles are more philosophical in nature, others more descriptive. There is no singular "evangelical position" regarding social assistance that could be gleaned from the articles, but a number of qualitative and quantitative observations are possible. First, a notable recurrence of a larger tension between individualism and compassion revealed itself in the articles and distinguished evangelical voices from more puritanically neoliberal ones (see Elisha 2008). Both sentiments — personal responsibility and compassion — are put forth as biblical mandates, and it is not a simple matter to reconcile them. Simply stating that individuals should fend for themselves seems to violate the ethic of compassion, while arguing that the state should provide for them seems to violate the ethic of individualism. The most common resolution to this ethical quandary is to begrudgingly acknowledge the necessity of the state for funding purposes but to aggressively promote evangelical alternatives to government welfare. The articles take the form of both descriptions of evangelical charities that were receiving government money, and more-philosophical editorials that stake out a more general position. In most, the prescribed model is one of autonomous evangelical FBOs receiving state money but with no oversight on how they performed their services, whom they hired, or whom they served (or refused to serve).

In a far more limited number of cases, the ethic of compassion led some to conclude that the state would be far more effective than small religious NGOs at promoting evangelical interests (namely, compassion for the poor). In the magazine's first article on the topic, for example, Joseph Dawson pens a stirring defense of democratic compassionate welfare-state government on biblical grounds. Dawson's analysis portrayed an almost Keynesian God and a manifestly Keynesian agenda for evangelicals: "Translated into particulars, governmental extension of love might cover social security, retirement benefits, assistance to the unemployed, aged and disabled, funds for veterans, housing, public health and care of the sick and mentally ill, soil conservation, agricultural subsidies, restraint of monopolies, regulation of public carriers, free education and many other benefits" (1957, 4). In this case, Dawson sees evangelical efforts as differing from those of government and suggests that Christians should be supportive of government efforts. But the response to Dawson's article and sentiment was overwhelmingly negative. In one of the many angry replies, the famously libertarian evangelical Howard Kershner writes succinctly, "We believe in extending Christian love, but we do not believe it can be done by the state. It can and should be done by individuals" (1957, 18). The sentiment of antigovernment individualism dramatically outweighs the Keynesian sentiments expressed by Dawson or implied by others. The casual assumption in most *Christianity Today* news articles and the overwhelming percentage of opinion pieces cast FBOs as either replacements for or enhancements of government-based welfare.

As mentioned earlier, ninety-two articles together provided an opportunity to create a code to assess how evangelical FBOs are being framed by *Christianity Today*. There are no instances in which such organizations are portrayed as serving as catalysts for progressive policy (FBOs as catalysts) or as extensions of the state through contractual relationships. There are also no instances in which such organizations are framed as doing the work that the state refused to do (FBOs as alternatives). FBOs as replacements and FBOs as enhancements are the only two motifs represented that match the typology discussed in chapter 1. Discussions of FBOs as replacements (30.4 percent) are not as common as those of FBOs as enhancements (69.6 percent), but where the FBO-as-replacement motif was expressed, it was expressed with passion. As one columnist pushing this perspective notes:

> The solution to the U.S. welfare-poverty crisis is to bring private initiative into partnership with government. One idea for privatizing public charity would allow individual taxpayers rather than politicians and bureaucrats to decide how a portion of welfare dollars is spent. A system would be set up by which individuals would allocate their tax dollars to a qualified charity, public or private. In this way, public and private charities would compete. (Matthews 1995)

In articles advocating the FBO-as-replacement model, direct subsidies through donations (that would be "unleashed" by lowering taxes) are the most common funding approach. But many questioned this approach, especially those working in actual FBOs, not least, as Everett Wilson (1996) points out, "because income from the private sector is too sporadic to provide for people on a sustaining basis." Primarily though not exclusively for this reason, most articles frame the normative ideal as FBOs as enhancements—dependent on a sustainable stream of funds from government but able to do as they please, serve (and deny) whomever they choose, and hire whom they wish without government interference. The obvious message of this framing is that, "yes, government welfare is a bad thing, but we need its money and have a solution that is better." Framing of this sort takes several forms. Most common are the various vignettes and features on actual FBOs, like Richmond, Virginia's STEP (Strategies to Elevate People) program, which mentored former welfare recipients in their efforts to escape poverty, or Lansing, Michigan's Love INC (Love in the Name of Christ), which links people in need with churches (Sherman 1999; Moore 1998). Government relationships—usually through funding—are duly acknowledged in such articles, but the FBOs in question are contrasted sharply with actual and hypothetical government-led efforts.

A number of qualitative themes are also worthy of note in these discussions. First, there is an interesting tension between compassion for those in need of welfare and judgment about how they found themselves in this situation. Arguably, this tension derives from the larger division within the evangelical community—whether to accept the quasi-socialistic principles of the social gospel or the extreme individualism of ideas like Reconstructionism. This tension is expressed most fully in the 1981 article that features famous evangelical commentators Ronald Sider and Gary North (Crowe 1981). Sider is known for arguing that government should ally with the church, and North is known for being an extreme Reconstructionist who doubts the authority of secular government to exist at all. Fragments of this tension have revealed themselves throughout the fifty-year discussion of welfare covered in *Christianity Today*. Philosophical statements suggesting that there is biblical authority for democratic, even secular government that provides aid for the poor are definitely to be found, as are an even greater number arguing that FBOs should be paid by the government to provide welfare. But these instances are always countered—sometimes through letters to the editor, sometimes through other articles, sometimes in the same article—by the highly individualist, welfareless state model for which the Religious Right (and neoliberals) have become famous. So, while it would be misleading to suggest that a singular position on welfare is expressed in the pages of *Christianity Today*, it would also be misleading to suggest that articles expressing sympathy for government or even for government funding are met with wide acceptance (or even ambivalence) in those same pages. Most articles, while self-consciously grappling with their "biblically mandated" responsibility to be compassionate to the poor, are also quite antistatist in general and almost completely opposed to (secular or government) welfare in particular.

This stance, when combined with the very present expressions of compassion for the poor, created a quandary for many authors. How, in particular, if evangelicals have the burden of compassion, are they to adopt a position that is self-consciously devoid of it (neoliberalism)? Many authors in the sample resolve this conflict through an appeal for paternalism toward the poor. In one of the more memorable examples of this, Amy Sherman (1999), a Manhattan Institute fellow, explains why many evangelicals were struggling with welfare reform. As the article begins laying the groundwork for denying welfare benefits to those in need, Sherman points out that some evangelicals "worried that it might be a case of weaning the baby off the bottle a little too quickly" (1999, 80). The parental metaphors do not stop there. Sherman goes on to celebrate Christian alternatives like a Mississippi program for churches to "adopt" former welfare recipients and offers childlike caricatures of former recipients who were finally relieved of their irresponsible ways. Though this is one of the more direct instances of paternalism, this theme recurs throughout the dataset.

It manifests itself in more subtle ways as well. First, there are numerous vignettes about the personal failings of welfare recipients—of their "unwillingness" (rather than inability) to find work or of their "shady" pasts. Though these portrayals are often followed by expressions of sympathy, there is a marked inclination toward emphasizing the individual causes of poverty in most articles. Second, the nature of many suggested evangelical alternatives also express a subtle form of paternalism. In one example, from a 1994 article, Andres Tapia discusses a program called "urban relocators," which involved (mostly white) evangelicals moving to inner-city communities in an effort to stabilize neighborhoods through their outreach. "We feel that moving to the inner city is a tangible expression of God's kingdom," observed one volunteer (50). The social purpose of this experiment was based on the idea that "the presence of middle-class families in the inner city [was] bringing real structural and personal changes that directly lower crime rates"(50). Even expressions of failing to achieve this agenda drip with paternalism. Noted one exasperated volunteer, "It was difficult to realize that even with all our education and zeal that there was a lot of stuff we can't do anything about" (51). Again, this is but one, albeit direct, example of the paternalism expressed in many of the articles about welfare. Welfare recipients are routinely framed as children, the government as a misguided parent, and evangelicals as responsible adults coming in to break the cycle of dependency.

The mid-1990s welfare reform debates were a lightning rod within the pages of *Christianity Today*. The subject, particularly conversations regarding Charitable Choice, are the focus of dozens of articles from the mid-1990s until the present. One interesting element of these discussions is that the broad-brush paternalism and antistatism evidenced before welfare reform are now more routinely countered by more-nuanced case studies explaining how and why efforts to end welfare may be misguided and even anti-Christian. Almost all the articles still "concede" that "government welfare had failed," and the antistatist diatribes by various evangelicals continue, but the larger debate also begins to include figures from actual FBO workers who knew firsthand what acting on the rhetoric would mean for their organizations. In one memorable example, Pastor Everett Wilson (1996) explains the problems that a proposal for welfare recipients to write a letter to their church asking for help before receiving aid would create for his congregation. He begins the piece by conceding the "obvious": "There is common agreement that welfare in the United States has become a monstrous consumer of public money from which society receives little payback," but he goes on to note that organizations like his do not have the resources to respond to such a transfer or to replace government. "Only the government," he states, "has the right and power to represent the whole society—to act on behalf of those left over and left out, and through taxation to require everyone to support its programs on their behalf." Thus it is one thing to transfer responsibility from government to churches with funding (FBOs as enhancements), but it is quite another to transfer financial responsibility to FBOs (FBOs as replacements).

Viewpoints like these crept back into the discussion within the pages of *Christianity Today* in the years following welfare reform, but even in these pieces governmental welfare is still framed as a serious problem. These perspectives are still in the minority. Broad-brush ideologues from the Manhattan Institute, Prison Fellowship, and other antistatist organizations still entered the debate and continued to push the FBOs-as-replacement motif at least as commonly as those who were daring to push the FBOs-as-enhancement, or even FBOs-as-extension, motif. Invoking the specter of Nazi Germany and Communist China, Charles Colson and Anne Morse have argued recently that Christians should be fearful of a future involving more welfare provision by the government and less by FBOs:

> Hannah Arendt, a brilliant 20th century political theorist, observed this phenomenon firsthand in Germany, describing in her classic book *The Origins of Totalitarianism* how totalitarian regimes succeed by the atomization of society—creating a mass of individuals isolated from the structures that hold civilized societies together. The result is that individuals are left to stand alone before the immense power of the state. America is far from this, but when I realize how easily it could happen, I am reminded of the unknown man who, in 1989, bravely stood alone in Tiananmen Square before a row of Chinese army tanks. Ensuring this doesn't happen in the U.S. is a solemn responsibility of every Christian. (Colson and Morse 2009)

Although not all commentators see such a narrow gap between government welfare provision and fascism, clearly the theme of small government neoliberalism is alive and well in the pages of *Christianity Today*. But it is noteworthy that the conversations since welfare reform have often been less ideological than this, and even periodically sympathetic to a strong governmental role in welfare.

In short, the dialogue about welfare in the pages of *Christianity Today* is more varied than it is in the NAE policy resolutions. There is a richer texture of actualized examples that surface, a wider variation in biblical verses used to justify various approaches, and a self-conscious desire to debate certain issues rather than to reach a singular resolution. That said, the emphasis in *Christianity Today* is still overwhelmingly antistatist in its presentation of government welfare. Government-led welfare is routinely cast as "inhumane," "inefficient," "expensive," and "unnecessary." But because the evangelical identity is self-consciously built, at least in part, on the idea of compassion, most critiques of government welfare are followed by or contrasted with the presentation of suitable alternatives. Most of these are, of course, framed as manifestly superior to government-led efforts. There is a great deal of variation in perspectives on the relationship that FBOs should have with government, but the idea of FBOs as an extension—a relatively uncontroversial contracting relationship—is never expressed, nor is the idea that government-led efforts might be better able to address certain problems. The overwhelming focus to situate FBOs as enhancements of government—organizations that can provide more-effective, efficient welfare, but that will rely in part on government funds. FBOs are routinely encouraged to demonstrate caution when entering relationships with government—accept government money, yes, but do not concede one inch to its nefariously secular requests.

COMPASSION AND THE AMERICAN RIGHT

The notion that private charity in general, and religious charities in particular, can and should provide welfare, rather than large governmental entities, is a durable cultural motif in the United States and certainly not unique to a single group. This notion has been common, perhaps central, to neoliberal ideology over the past thirty years. The literature on actualized FBOs complicates both the fantasy of such organizations replacing the state (by demonstrating, among other factors, capacity constraints), and the actualized extent to which replacement has already happened (by demonstrating that FBOs function in a variety of ways that complicate or even contradict this notion). The presence of this theme within evangelical texts is important for a number of reasons. First, unlike the general antistatism of the neoliberal/economic conservative branch of the American Right, the identity of many evangelicals ostensibly coalesces around the theme of compassion — particularly for the poor. This theme makes antiwelfarist diatribes discursively challenging for evangelicals. Arguing, for example, that the welfare state be abolished is difficult (though some have tried, as noted above) without coming across as mean spirited, and worse, for this audience, blasphemous. The discursive contortions required for evangelical voices to be simultaneously antiwelfarist and yet also present a compassionate stance toward the poor are interesting in their own right. Most often this is accomplished through the presentation of evangelical alternatives — often, though not always, FBOs that receive some government funding but that determine whom they serve and how they serve them, without government oversight.

Second, evangelical pronouncements are interesting because they still have considerable political influence. As scholars of the American Right have shown, efforts to fuse disparate wings of the conservative movement in the United States have been challenging. So discursive efforts of this sort — narratives that weave together evangelical identity and neoliberal politics — are enormously useful for building political coalitions. Indeed, one might argue that this particular set of narratives — those dealing with welfare — has been responsible for keeping the Republicans in power from the early 1980s until very recently. One might also argue that such narratives can only mask inherent contradictions that seem to be currently splintering the Right. Third, such narratives offer a window into the political capacity of biblical legitimacy. To be sure, the ideas of self-help, small government, and FBO welfare are not unique to evangelicals. Many groups in the United States hold one or more of these tenets as central points of identity. But by the same token, the application of scripture — as is so often the case in both the NAE policy resolutions and *Christianity Today* articles—can lend a retroactive theological legitimacy to matters that might have originated firmly within secular arenas. Welfare reform, for example, is much harder to defend to self-identified evangelicals as compassionate if one uses the indifferent language of the CATO Institute to justify it.

Invoking biblical verses not only has the potential to bring together evangelical Christians and neoliberals, it lends a credibility and compassion to the issue that can distract from the most callous features of related policy. Hayek may have been a persuasive man, but his words do not carry the same weight as the Bible among self-identified evangelicals. Evangelical texts, such as those featured in this chapter, are of course only one piece in a complicated, multilayered puzzle. Examining such voices can systematically illustrate the contours of an idealized welfare model being promoted by a very powerful group and help in speculating about the extent to which this model serves as political glue binding two very different factions of the American Right.

CHAPTER FOUR

Mainstream Jesus Economics

Identifying religious neoliberalism in the words of Acton Institute ideologues or mainstream evangelicals may be an important step in understanding its ideational nuances, but it is hardly proof that anything wider has evolved to influence public policy or the ethos about welfare in general. For that, a consideration of secular and mainstream media is needed. The challenge with such a focus, of course, is that one is unlikely to find broad, programmatic texts outlining how a merger of religion and neoliberalism would look — even if that were something editors would approve. Religious neoliberalism, if it exists at all in the mainstream, appears in a fragmentary form, and these fragments are glued to other ideas, inclinations, and biases. In short, while it is challenging to find religious neoliberalism in the mainstream, it is important to do so if one seeks to suggest that its presence is more than a fantasy of self-professed religious neoliberals.

In the attempt to illuminate religious neoliberalism's mainstream currents, this chapter focuses on the presentation of Habitat for Humanity within a variety of mainstream newspapers. Though once an obscure organization, Habitat is now referred to constantly in the press — so much so that there has been a noticeable decrease in the number of contextualizing background statements on the organization (since the average reader is already familiar with it). As one article analyzed for this book notes succinctly in place of a background explanation: "You [already] know Habitat for Humanity" (*Toronto Star* 2004). But what exactly does the public know about Habitat for Humanity? Surely, most know it is a housing provider that relies on volunteer labor. Surely, most know that its building sites provide a popular photo-op for politicians. And most probably know that it is affiliated with religious groups. Some may even know that its founder once deemed its approach "Jesus economics" — a faith-based alternative to government-funded housing. Many might also be aware that it refuses to take government money (even though it has softened this stance in recent years). It is impossible to determine exactly what knowledge and preconceived notions influence individuals' perceptions of each Habitat reference (or any reference for that matter), and that is certainly not the intent here. But much, I contend, can be learned from systematically studying the way religious nonprofits like Habitat for Humanity are discursively portrayed in the media. In particular it is clear that, whatever the specific intent of Habitat volunteers, donors, or recipients, the organization is increasingly framed, in an almost commonsensical way, as an alternative to government efforts in the housing sector. Sometimes this framing is direct and ideological, as in a number of *Wall Street Journal* editorials, but more often than not it is subtle and implied, as in the hundreds of instances of Habitat being positively, and perhaps innocently, juxtaposed against the efforts of government, or of government being cast as a nefarious obstacle to the venerated organization.

The observation that Habitat is framed in such a way widens the narrative of this book from a story of think-tank ideologues and true believers to one in which the ideas of such figures intersect with similar ideas that may have a different source of inspiration. Put simply, the almost unchallenged veneration of Habitat for Humanity — an openly religious, albeit pluralist, housing nonprofit that refuses to take government money — as a universally respected alternative to government-led housing efforts provides at least a clue that although religious neoliberalism as a systematic ideological project may be marginal, some of the assumptions flowing from this worldview are very present in the U.S. mainstream political sphere.

HABITAT FOR HUMANITY

Habitat for Humanity was created in Americus, Georgia, in 1976 by Millard Fuller, an evangelical corporate lawyer who had grown disaffected with his life (Fuller and Scott 1980). He established the organization as one that relied on volunteers to help build and finance houses for those in need. In order to qualify for a house, recipients had to contribute labor toward its construction (initially five hundred hours, now as low as three hundred in some locations) and adhere to various credit and criminal background checks. To Fuller, the organization is built first and foremost upon religious principles. As he notes in a 2006 discussion of the organization: "I placed a sign in a window in Americus, Georgia, proclaiming the opening of Habitat for Humanity. This is God's work. Habitat for Humanity is a Christian ministry created to witness to the gospel of Jesus Christ. Churches, therefore, are natural and primary partners" (49). Though the range of volunteers and housing recipients is relatively pluralistic (see Hays 2002 for an interesting discussion of this), Fuller himself ties the organization explicitly to Christian roots. In later work on the organization, the phrase "Jesus economics" emerged (used also by Fuller himself) to describe its foundation (Baggett 2001). As of 2008, the organization had built over 250,000 units worldwide and had affiliates in ninety countries (Habitat for Humanity International 2008).

Habitat for Humanity has become the favorite charity of a number of high-profile politicians and celebrities, perhaps none more committed than Jimmy Carter. Carter has helped make the organization famous since leaving office in 1981, volunteering to help build its houses in many parts of the world. It is an oft-repeated myth — one that is pleasantly corrected by Habitat staff — that Carter is the founder of the organization. Habitat has also become very popular with antigovernment politicians like Newt Gingrich. Until very recently, it refused to take government funds at all. It still refuses to take direct government contributions; it will only accept land and other in-kind contributions from government (Nagel 1998).

Recently, the organization experienced a high-profile shake-up in which Millard Fuller was fired as CEO by the board of directors for allegations of sexual harassment (*New York Times* 2005). Fuller has gone on to start a competing organization, The Fuller Center for Housing. Beneath the salacious details of Fuller's exit is a systematic transition to a more "professional" nonprofit organization. Habitat's new directors are now somewhat more interested in working with governments and engaged in a much larger marketing campaign than previously. Recent examples of the latter include high-profile celebrity involvement in the organization, glossy advertisements in magazines, and national television commercials in the United States and Canada designed, first and foremost, to bring in funds, but also to enhance the organization's "brand" as an alternative to welfare.[1] This departs radically from the original highly decentralized, almost folksy model envisaged and built by Fuller.

Why focus on Habitat for Humanity as a case for this book? First, surprisingly little academic material has been written about this organization, and nothing (to my knowledge) has been written on this particular angle. Notable exceptions include an article written by R. Allen Hays (2002) arguing that Habitat for Humanity can have a key role in enhancing social capital, and a book by Jerome P. Baggett (2001) suggesting that the organization inspires a sort of public religion for all. Books by current and former directors (Fuller and Scott 1980; Reckford 2007; Frye 1996) are interesting reads but understandably not intended to critically evaluate Habitat's positioning within the wider political economy. Some notable exceptions include works by Ananta Kumar Giri (2002), Paul Leonard (2006), and Rodger Trigg and Fabian Nabangi (1995), which all provide analyses that begin to address Habitat's limitations but are generally uncritical of its central mission. In part, the effusive nature of coverage about Habitat is an expression of how widely respected the organization is among groups of varying perspectives. But this does not change the relative dearth of basic, critical scholarship on the topic.

Second, Habitat is worthy of examination because it is difficult to imagine another organization in relation to which public perception of its capacity differs so radically from reality. The public perception of the organization — reflected in the articles discussed below — ranges from "could be helpful for ameliorating the housing problem" to "should be the central vehicle for dismantling government-led housing programs." This is radically different from the message put forth by Habitat for Humanity itself. Though most Habitat officials are very positive about their organization, most are also very careful to clarify the organization's limitations in direct conversations, press releases, or website material. Many emphasize the fact that the organization is much too small and disparately organized (even after the reorganization) to assist all those in need or even a sizable portion of them. Habitat officials were interviewed as part of this study, and public statistics were examined to obtain some measurement of capacity. Habitat International officials noted that the figures were not kept centrally, but local affiliates revealed their own numbers in some cases. Even a limited sample of responses underscores the capacity limitations of the organization.[2] I report these figures not to minimize Habitat's importance but to highlight its inherent capacity limitations and contrast them with its "potential" as expressed through the mainstream press. This tension between the capacity limitations of the organization, its branding practices that tend to obfuscate them, and a public dialogue that positions the organization as a potential salve for the housing crisis creates an interesting space within which to ask these questions. We can be reasonably certain that constant references to Habitat for Humanity as an alternative to government are not based on a systematic consideration of the topic. Such references are either a fantasy of religious neoliberals, a casual political jab at a common enemy (government-funded housing), or misinformed.

GAUGING "THE MAINSTREAM"

In order to study the framing of the organization, a content analysis was performed on all articles featuring the phrase "Habitat for Humanity" in either the title or the text from six selected newspapers from 1976 to present: the *New York Times*, the *Wall Street Journal*, and the *Washington Times* from the United States; and the *Globe and Mail*, the *National Post*, and the *Toronto Star* from

Canada.[3] These six newspapers were deliberately chosen to span the mainstream political spectrum and serve as suitable representatives from Canada and the United States so that geography and political orientation could eventually be factored into the analysis.[4] Adding Canada to the picture allows for a control case to evaluate the novelty of processes occurring in the United States.

Three newspapers from the United States were chosen for the analysis to maximize the political spectrum of nationally focused newspapers. The *New York Times* is one of the most widely respected newspapers in the United States. It aims for a balance of regional, national, and international coverage. I understand it to be a "liberal" newspaper both because of its popularity among liberals and, just as importantly, because it is so reviled by conservatives. The *Wall Street Journal* has a more specialized but slightly larger readership. It is a business-oriented publication but does provide national political coverage from a perspective that is understood by this author as "economic conservative" or "neoliberal." The *Washington Times* is the newest of the U.S. publications selected and was chosen because it is an openly conservative publication (both socially and economically) that provides some national coverage.

Three publications were also chosen from Canada, where the political spectrum and its media representatives are somewhat different. The *Toronto Star* is the largest paper (by readership) in Canada and is generally considered a "liberal" (center-left) publication. But the *Star* is also more regionally focused than any of the other choices in this study, so the *Globe and Mail* was also included. The *Globe and Mail* does not have a strong political identity within Canadian society, but it is a highly regarded mainstream publication included here to avoid overrepresenting stories about Toronto. Finally, the *National Post* is a nationally focused newspaper owned by the conservative icon Conrad Black. It has been a national newspaper since 1998 but existed in a previous incarnation as the *Financial Post*, a business-focused publication that generally held the same economically conservative viewpoint as the *National Post*. There are no perfect equivalents to the *Washington Times* in Canada, as social conservatism does not occupy the same place in the Canadian public culture as it does in the United States.

All articles from these six newspapers (beginning in 1976) that included the phrase "Habitat for Humanity" in either the title or the body were retrieved and compiled into a searchable database. This yielded an initial sample of 1,427 articles (see table 4.1). Each article was then read, analyzed, and coded. The first step was to eliminate all incidental references to Habitat for Humanity so that the focus could remain on the most substantive references, yielding a total of 532 articles.[5] These were then read for qualitative meaning—focusing on

TABLE 4.1 Annual totals for all news articles that contain "Habitat for Humanity" in the text or title, selected newspapers, 1976–2007

YEAR	*New York Times*	*Wall Street Journal*	*Washington Times*	*Toronto Star*	*National/ Financial Post*	*Globe and Mail*	TOTAL
2007	49	7	8	37	18	34	153
2006	38	12	11	41	17	18	137
2005	29	10	7	43	8	14	111
2004	18	2	11	59	6	13	109
2003	28	2	13	42	9	14	108
2002	28	7	16	54	3	4	112
2001	33	10	24	20	5	5	97
2000	32	12	18	31	6	4	103
1999	22	3	20	16	3	4	68
1998	11	6	20	8	0	3	48
1997	32	2	24	10	2	2	72
1996	16	10	25	6	0	1	58
1995	18	5	31	9	1	2	66
1994	15	2	12	8	0	1	38
1993	6	3	6	10	3	6	34
1992	10	3	10	8	0	4	35
1991	8	2	4	0	0	0	14
1990	4	1	4	1	0	1	11
1989	5	1	—	4	0	1	11
1988	2	1	—	0	0	2	5
1987	2	1	—	2	0	0	5
1986	7	0	—	3	0	0	10
1985	4	1	—	0	0	1	6
1984	13	1	—	—	—	—	14
1983	0	0	—	—	—	—	0
1982	1	0	—	—	—	—	1
1981	1	0	—	—	—	—	1
1980	0	0	—	—	—	—	0
1979	0	0	—	—	—	—	0
1978	0	0	—	—	—	—	0
1977	0	0	—	—	—	—	0
1976	0	0	—	—	—	—	0
TOTAL	432	104	264	412	81	134	1427

TABLE 4.2 Examples of religious and secular descriptors for Habitat for Humanity in the newspaper text

EXAMPLES OF RELIGIOUS DESCRIPTORS	EXAMPLES OF SECULAR DESCRIPTORS
"a religious charity"; "an ecumenical house-building group"; "an ecumenical Christian organization"; "an ecumenical organization"; "a faith-based organization"; "a single-issue evangelical group"; "a Christian group"; "a faith-based NGO"; "a Georgia-based Christian group"	"a social service"; "a public-private partnership"; "a charity"; "a nonprofit organization"; "a low-income housing initiative"; "a volunteer-based nonprofit builder"; "a housing provider"; "a network of volunteers"; "a partnership venture of businesses, individual donors, and volunteers"; "housing advocacy organization"; "volunteer home-building group"; "that Jimmy Carter group"; "a good social cancer spreading lot by lot"; "a good cause"; "an international self-help organization"

context, the way Habitat is framed as an organization, and political perspectives expressed intentionally and unintentionally using the organization as a vehicle. The articles were then coded and counted according to their framing of Habitat's religiosity (table 4.2) and of its position vis-à-vis government. The latter involved examining the extent to which Habitat for Humanity was framed as either a replacement for or a direct challenge to interventionist government. For the quantitative portion of this study, only those articles in which a clear positioning of Habitat for Humanity could be discerned were included. This positioning occurred in three principal ways that are sketched in table 4.3 and explained in detail below.

Habitat for Humanity as sanctified replacement

It is difficult, if not impossible, to comprehensively summarize the contents of 532 different news articles, from two different countries and offering a variety of political perspectives, but a few themes emerged as most salient for this discussion. First, as tables 4.1 and 4.4 suggest, the sheer number of references to Habitat for Humanity has increased steadily over time. Very few articles about the organization existed in the late 1970s and early 1980s, but by the 1990s all selected newspapers displayed substantial coverage. Hidden beneath these numbers is the fact that the organization was typically referred to more casually, with no explanation of its origins or purpose, by the late 1990s and early 2000s — surely a sign that Habitat had achieved a "brand value" or had

TABLE 4.3 Examples of Habitat for Humanity deployed as a "replacement" or "solution" to "government failure"

REPRESENTATION	EXAMPLE ARTICLE	REPRESENTATIVE QUOTE (*from example article*)
Habitat for Humanity as a "solution" for "government failure"	"Privatize the Welfare State" (*Wall Street Journal* 2006)	"The idea, endorsed by GOP presidential challenger Robert Dole, is simple enough. Give money to a private charity whose work you support and the government will give you a tax credit equal to your donation. 'It would present Americans with a stark choice,' Mr. Dole said recently. 'Give your money to the Department of Housing and Urban Development, or give it to Habitat for Humanity . . . to big government, or to Big Brothers and Big Sisters.'"
Habitat for Humanity as an antidote to welfare state	"Habitat for Humanity Picks New Leader amid Turmoil" (*New York Times* 2005)	"Nicknamed by an anonymous volunteer 'The Ministry of the Hammer,' Habitat for Humanity International, founded in 1976 in Americus, Ga., uses no public funds. It is underwritten by churches, synagogues, individuals and corporations in 500 American cities and 45 foreign countries."
The local managerialist state as an obstacle to Habitat for Humanity	"Building Hope: The Star to Join with Habitat in Project during Pope's Visit" (*Toronto Star* 2002a)	"Despite the fact the houses are sold at cost to people who wouldn't otherwise be able to buy them, the city doesn't give Habitat a blanket exemption on development fees."

TABLE 4.4 **Temporal change in the deployment of Habitat for Humanity as a "solution" to "government failure"**

YEAR	TOTAL ARTICLES	SUBSTANTIVE REFERENCES	PERCENT OF TOTAL	HABITAT AS A "SOLUTION" TO "GOVERNMENT FAILURE"	PERCENT OF SUBSTANTIVE REFERENCES
2007	153	54	35.3	12	22.2
2006	137	43	31.4	1	2.3
2005	111	40	36.0	6	15.0
2004	109	44	40.4	4	9.1
2003	108	48	44.4	3	6.3
2002	112	41	36.6	12	29.3
2001	97	31	32.0	3	9.7
2000	103	34	33.0	5	14.7
1999	68	14	20.6	1	7.1
1998	48	16	33.3	1	6.3
1997	72	23	31.9	4	17.4
1996	58	18	31.0	4	22.2
1995	66	25	37.9	10	40.0
1994	38	13	34.2	0	—
1993	34	21	61.8	3	14.3
1992	35	18	51.4	1	5.6
1991	14	5	35.7	1	20.0
1990	11	7	63.6	0	—
1989	11	7	63.6	1	14.3
1988	5	3	60.0	0	—
1987	5	5	100.0	1	20.0
1986	10	6	60.0	0	—
1985	6	6	100.0	0	—
1984	14	8	57.1	0	—
1983	0	0	—	0	—
1982	1	1	100.0	0	—
1981	1	1	100.0	0	—
1980	0	0	—	0	—
1979	0	0	—	0	—
1978	0	0	—	0	—
1977	0	0	—	0	—
1976	0	0	—	0	—
TOTAL	1427	532	37.3	73	13.7

become a known entity within the wider public culture. A 2004 *Toronto Star* article even quipped about this familiarity in a characteristically effusive way: "You know Habitat. . . . They buy land and build affordable housing for families in need, using donated material and volunteer labour; some professional and some amateur. . . . Sounds simple, sounds pragmatic, sounds brilliant." Almost all references to Habitat were as positive as this one, regardless of the time, country, or political inclinations of the newspaper. In only 25 cases (less than 5 percent) was Habitat for Humanity framed negatively at all, and in even fewer cases was it framed as inferior to government or government-provided housing. The praise ranged from implied to utterly effusive. The vast majority of articles praised some aspect of Habitat, ranging from the "heroic" volunteers, to the organization itself, to how it must contend with governments at various levels inappropriately stepping in the way.

Table 4.4 displays the incidence of articles in which Habitat was deployed as a "solution" to "government failure." The frequency of articles in which Habitat was cast as such ranges from 6.3 to 40 percent of the articles for a given year. This contrasts sharply with the cases (overall only 25) in which Habitat was framed as inferior to government (0.7 to 20 percent for a given year). But even this contrast grossly understates the level of antiwelfarism in Habitat references, for two reasons: (1) it excludes incidental mentions (removed from the sample) encompassing both Habitat and antiwelfare sentiment, which were somewhat common in the *Wall Street Journal* and the *Washington Times*; and (2) it excludes all cases where Habitat was, by implication (but not directly), framed as a replacement for government (discussed below). Nevertheless, table 4.4 provides a basic metric of change over time.

Habitat for Humanity as a direct "solution" to "government failure"

In several cases, particularly in editorials and op-eds, the organization was directly cast as an alternative to a vilified welfare state. Not surprisingly, most, though not all, of these editorials appeared in the *Washington Times* and the *Wall Street Journal* (though none appeared in the *National Post*, the other ostensibly conservative paper in this study). Also not surprisingly, articles of this sort were more common around sea-changing conservative moments in the recent past—the Republican takeover of the U.S. Congress in 1994 and the Bush administration entering office in 2000, in particular.[6]

In one of the earliest examples of this framing, *Wall Street Journal* reporter Virginia Postrel lamented the affordability crisis facing many American families in the late 1980s (*Wall Street Journal* 1987). She framed the problem succinctly and then immediately moved on to argue that government programs were impotent to solve the problem:

> The lack of affordable housing is particularly acute (and well-known) among poorer families, especially those relying on one income, because as household income goes down, the percentage devoted to housing rises. Yet traditional government remedies—housing projects, subsidies—have largely failed, tearing down neighborhoods, uprooting the elderly, creating ghettos of age or class, and costing far more per unit than quality can justify or political realities will allow.

Lest the reader think that hers was the ideology of mean-spiritedness, she then moved onto "solutions." First, she emphasized the general approach that was needed: "The alternative to government programs is not abandonment of the poor. Taking advantage of changing demographics, we can go a long way toward improving American housing by encouraging more efficient use of existing buildings—at a savings of a third or more over the cost of new construction. In many cases, this encouragement need consist simply of loosening land-use regulations or freeing up unused government-owned buildings." Then, she began to list specific instances of this idea in practice, including a prominent example involving Habitat for Humanity:

> On New York's Lower East Side, the Christian group Habitat for Humanity purchased a six-story abandoned building from the city for $19,000. The building, says the project's executive director Rob DeRocker, "had been vacant for five years, except for junkies and homeless people. Even the rats had moved out." Using donations and volunteer labor, the group renovated the building to produce 19 units that will be sold at no profit through 30-year, no-interest mortgages.

Not limiting herself to simply a critique of government intervention in general, she then went on to point out how the local managerialist state had ruined Habitat's original plan for the project: "Ironically, Habitat originally had planned to renovate a smaller, formerly church-owned building. But two days after Habitat signed the contract to take it over, the city condemned the building to make way for public housing."[7] Later, just after the Republican takeover of Congress, an invited editorial in the same newspaper by noted conservative economist Howard Husock extended this theme and logic (*Wall Street Journal* 1995). He framed the organization in starkly ideological terms. Habitat is a good thing, he argued, but it should stay away from government, and government away from it: "It is one thing, however, to approve of an organization—and another thing to approve federal funds for it. One must ask, Will such funds be good for Habitat in the long run? More broadly, the implicit question here is one about the stance government should take to ensure a healthy independent (i.e., nonprofit, charitable) sector. . . . The broader question here is that of government influence on the nonprofit sector." According to Husock, government should do little more than provide tax breaks for people who want to donate to Habitat for Humanity. From his perspective, subsidies are misguided at best, and at worst, they distort the mission of such organizations. He (and former Habitat director Millard Fuller, who is quoted) ended by framing the government as a "snake" of which the organization should be wary: "If this legislation passes, Habitat for Humanity will have to hope that as an organization with its own distinct and clear sense of mission it can avoid the distractions that come with chasing government grants. 'The trick,' Mr. Fuller says of government aid, 'is to dance close to the snake but not get bit.' He may be underestimating the snake." Husock penned another critique of the government using Habitat for Humanity as an example in 2006 (*Wall Street Journal* 2006). His approach was paralleled by similar efforts from other authors, primarily in the *Washington Times*. In general, though, brazenly framing Habitat as a replacement for the welfare state was the least-used, if most direct, device for highlighting "government failure." More often, the organization was simply framed as an antidote to some aspect of the welfare state.

Habitat for Humanity as an antidote to the welfare state

Representing Habitat as a positive alternative to some aspect of the welfare state — real or perceived — was more common and widespread than deploying it as a putative replacement. Moreover, this theme — framing Habitat as a partial antidote — was not limited to the *Wall Street Journal* and the *Washington Times*. By far the most common example of this representation was the talking point that "Habitat is not a handout, but rather a hand up." This phraseology derives from a Habitat promotional point that has been employed very successfully in raising funds and motivating volunteers. It is also very clear that it is a thinly veiled critique of "handouts" from the government.

Throughout the 1980s and early 1990s, most mentions of the language of "handouts" were simply quotes given by Habitat directors to the media.[8] In one (of many) examples, Carol Casperson, former executive director of the Washington, D.C., Habitat affiliate, noted in a mid-1990s *Washington Times* (1995) article, "'We think people should get a hand up, not a hand out.'" Similarly, in a *Toronto Star* (1993) article quoting Jimmy Carter: "Habitat homes are not handouts, such as government-subsidized housing." Increasingly over time, this talking point melted into the phraseology of the reporters and columnists more directly. The *Toronto Star* was the most frequent user of this approach. In 1995, it described the organization, which at the time was relatively new to the area, as follows: "The Toronto chapter of Habitat for Humanity is a non-profit charity. . . . Their goal is to give families a hand up, not a handout, . . . [and to] . . . look for businesses, religious and community groups and concerned individuals willing to help out with financial support." Later, in 2002, an editorial in the *Toronto Star* (2002c) by Greater Toronto Area Homebuilders Association president Sheldon Libfeld noted with perfect talking-point discipline that "Habitat's philosophy is based on housing the working poor by providing a hand up, not a handout." Whatever the intent of this language, the notion had transformed from a promotional talking point into an uncontroversial descriptor of the organization used by independent observers.

More subtle and common was the simple emphasis on "sweat equity" in describing Habitat's mission and projects. "Sweat equity" in this instance referred to the work requirement that each family must complete toward the construction of their home. Fully 96 (18 percent) of the 532 articles that substantively referenced the organization also emphasized or repeated the phrase "sweat equity." In many cases, this was not coded in the research tabulation as a "solution" to government failure, because it was just mentioned ostensibly as a fact (for example, *Toronto Star* 2002d). But it is worth mentioning here to point out that the phrase has become firmly hinged to Habitat, and it is not a stretch to suggest that simply invoking the phrase is a subtle critique of those programs that ostensibly do not require this type of input, such as (most of) those delivered by government and secular nonprofits. Moreover, the language of "sweat equity" was also often coupled with quotes or language that more directly critiqued the welfare state or its perceived imperfections. Quoting Neil Heatherington, Toronto Habitat CEO, the *Toronto Star* (2007) noted, "Families don't need charity, and they need co-workers, not case workers." As in most articles of this kind, no effort was made to counter this implied criticism elsewhere, so it was left unchallenged.

Invoking the language of "sweat equity" and "handouts" was not the only method of highlighting the differences between Habitat's product and state-delivered housing. Sometimes the contrast was made more directly through vignettes of Habitat "rescuing" people from publicly subsidized housing. In one example, the *Toronto Star* (2005a) celebrated the completion of a Habitat home for a family in Toronto while at the same time contrasting it with the "cramped" conditions in publicly subsidized housing: "Before moving into the two-storey home a month ago, which is nestled in the McLevin Woods area of Scarborough, Stewart and her children spent many years crammed into a two-bedroom apartment in a Metro Housing building." A similar example can be found in a *Globe and Mail* (2005) article printed in the same year: "Poised to move in next month, most of the new homeowners tell a similar tale. More than half are immigrants living in public housing. All work and have been poor for most of their lives." It is undoubtedly true that Habitat homes are, on average, much nicer than government-provided housing (in both countries), but continuing to invoke this idea without clarification that Habitat is in no position to replace or even meaningfully supplement government-run public housing systems has the collective effect of normalizing Habitat as an antidote to "government failure."

The local managerialist state as an obstacle to Habitat for Humanity

Editorials that positioned Habitat as a "replacement" and articles that overemphasized an implied critique of the welfare state were not the only means of emphasizing "government failure." A third category of articles positioned the local state (usually, though not always, the municipal government) as an obstacle to Habitat's efforts. Perhaps because it is the most locally focused of the newspapers analyzed here, the *Toronto Star* featured the most articles with this approach. Overall, this theme tended to take three related forms: (1) criticizing government for having onerous building rules; (2) criticizing local government bureaucracy for slowing the approval of existing applications by Habitat; or (3) criticizing how a proposed government policy would disrupt the efforts of Habitat.

In an example representative of the first form, the *Toronto Star* (2002b) lamented delays in Habitat construction related to a government workers union: "The dreams of 14 low-income families to move into their own homes have been put on hold because of bureaucratic delays. . . . The delay has also put at risk hundreds of thousands of dollars in donations for the Habitat for Humanity project and leaves 2,000 volunteers idle." A couple of years later, in the same newspaper (*Toronto Star* 2004), the City of Toronto was criticized for slowing a project because of its building laws: "Today's hitch: the city has asked for a minor but annoying change. The building inspector requires a thicker beam in the front of the house, under the deck. This means some of the work that was done yesterday must be undone, and done again." Such comments routinely went unchallenged. There was rarely a counterquote provided by a city official or a counterargument to balance this perspective.[9] The frequency of such comments collectively framed Habitat as a benevolent force and government as a source of annoyance, inefficiency, or worse.

The second form of the local managerialist state critique targeted larger-scaled policies that were perceived to inhibit the general activities of the organization. An illuminating *New York Times* (2000) article covered a battle between local environmentalists and affordable-housing activists regarding proposed antisprawl legislation. The interesting element of the article for the purposes of this study was the way Habitat was framed vis-à-vis the state governments of Arizona and Colorado:

> Until this year, Habitat for Humanity affiliates in Arizona and Colorado never felt a need to get involved in a political fight. . . . In one of the most far-reaching efforts yet to curb suburban sprawl, ballot initiatives in both states proposed giving voters an unprecedented level of power to designate wide swaths of land off limits to new housing. . . . Officials with Habitat, which builds low-income housing for needy families, feared that the measures would drive up the cost of land and "basically shut down our ability to acquire land and lots for growth," said Chris Wolf, the organization's director in Phoenix.

Though other figures were quoted in the article who supported the proposed legislation, no direct rebuttal to the notion that Habitat's efforts would be stymied was offered. Rather, in this article (like others), it was considered axiomatic that Habitat's efforts would become more challenging, and that this was simply an inevitable corollary to addressing other concerns.

Overall, Habitat was more often framed as a benevolent force impeded, in one way or another, by "misguided" interventionist local governments than as a "healthy partner" of government. This tended to be the case more in the *Toronto Star*, which had more local coverage, but was also found frequently in the *Washington Times*, the *Globe and Mail*, and the *New York Times*. This theme was rare in the *Wall Street Journal* and completely absent in the *National Post*.

Implicitly positioning Habitat for Humanity as a solution to "government failure"

Though there was no systematic effort to code articles as presenting "solutions" to "government failure" in this study, several indirect means of glamorizing the Habitat model were apparent. The motivations behind such themes varied, and as such, it would be improper to categorize them with those listed in the preceding section, but they are important collectively for venerating the Habitat model. When coupled with direct attacks on government intervention in housing and the minimal coverage of Habitat's capacity limitations, such themes contribute to the normalization of Habitat as an alternative to state-delivered housing.

One of the most common themes of this sort was the exaggeration of Habitat's scope or influence, either in the lives of those it formally serves or in society at large. A *Globe and Mail* article from 2004, for example, portrayed Habitat as a vehicle for enabling "families [to] escape from the cycle of poverty." A *Toronto Star* article (2002e) claimed even more comprehensive effects: "The concept of Habitat is simple. It raises money to build simple, decent houses for families living below the poverty line. . . . The net result is manifold: Cycles of poverty are broken, self-esteem is restored, children live in homes, not hovels." There are many reasons to be positive about the organization, from many different perspectives, so it is not surprising to find this level of enthusiasm. But the important point here is that when this effusive coverage of Habitat's positive attributes is coupled with the aforementioned direct challenges to interventionist government, on the one hand, and the lack of coverage highlighting the organization's limitations (or interventionist government's virtues), on the other, the net effect is one in which Habitat emerges as a discursive alternative to the welfare state.

Another common theme of this sort was the glamorization of volunteering, achieved, for example, through dozens of articles that covered a famous person volunteering or participating in some way with Habitat for Humanity. Many articles highlighted the participation of celebrities (Jon Bon Jovi, Paris Hilton, Amy Grant); politicians (Barack Obama, George W. Bush, Bill and Hillary Clinton, Al Gore, Newt Gingrich, former Louisiana governor Kathleen Blanco, Virginia governor Tim Kaine, and of course Jimmy Carter and his wife, Rosalynn); heads of state (South Korean president Kim Dae-Jung); royalty (Queen Elizabeth, Prince Edward and wife, Sophie Rhys-Jones); and famous clergy (Pope John Paul II). But not all volunteering articles highlighted the experiences of the famous. Many also had the effect of venerating the everyday volunteer as mildly heroic. In a characteristic article of this sort in 1998, the *New York Times* covered a Habitat project in New York by emphasizing the sacrifice of the volunteer experience itself: "About 50 people huddled in the dark basement of the new construction, the only place on the lot that offered any shelter. And while the intense rain crept in through a dozen dripping cracks and continued to soak the piles of plywood and stacks of two-by-fours, an invocation with a different cadence was brought forth into the room." Similarly, many articles covered the experience of volunteering for Habitat as a vacation, what one newspaper called "voluntourism." The practice was venerated as something that good people did on vacation (for example, *Toronto Star* 2006) or even as an honorable dating opportunity. Many Habitat affiliates have organized "singles build" programs that require volunteers to bring a date. Many of these were advertised and covered, especially in the *Toronto Star*, the *Globe and Mail*, and the *New York Times*. For example: "Singles are invited to build new relationships and help out Habitat for Humanity Toronto on Saturday. At the third annual Valentine singles build, 30 volunteers will swing hammers and shoot nail guns at the McLevin Woods site, near Neilson Rd. and McLevin Ave. in Scarborough, to help build a house for a low-income family. . . . Games and contests will also take place throughout the day to encourage people to get to know each other" (*Toronto Star* 2005b). Finally, a sizable number of articles featured the voluntary contributions of the corporate community, either firms themselves or their leaders. Most often this simply consisted of mentioning the contribution of a given corporation. Examples included Sprint Canada, the Greater Toronto Area Homebuilders Association, the Toronto Maple Leafs, Dewalt, Dow Chemical, RBC Financial, Home Depot, and CIL Paint, among many others. In one of the more humorous (in its efforts to humanize the volunteers) articles highlighting corporate benevolence, the *Wall Street Journal* (2002) described the scene when executives met in Baltimore to volunteer at a Habitat site. Executives emerged from limousines to volunteer on a Habitat site and attracted attention for their sacrifice. Glamorizing volunteering, whether by corporations or otherwise, is hardly a malevolent thing to do. I raise the issue here to argue that it contributes to a narrative that normalizes Habitat (and models like it) as an honorable alternative to the welfare state.

UNDERSTANDING DIFFERENCES IN HABITAT AS REPLACEMENT

While this analysis has illustrated how Habitat is portrayed in general, and to a certain extent how this has varied over time, it does not yet tell us how these themes vary across political orientation. Are they the product of a single newspaper, political perspective, or national context? To address these questions, more systematic comparisons were made across the sample. To determine the extent to which aforementioned discursive framings were attributable to the political inclinations of the newspapers, a series of chi-square analyses were performed. Chi-square allows for the statistical comparison of categorical data between actual and expected (based on their proportion in the sample) frequencies. Several chi-square comparisons were made to explore whether the framing of "government failures" differed between "liberal" (*New York Times* and *Toronto Star*) and "conservative" newspapers (*National Post*, *Wall Street Journal*, and *Washington Times*).[10]

Table 4.5 compares the basic frequencies of Habitat framing (vis-à-vis interventionist government) between "liberal" and "conservative" newspapers.

TABLE 4.5 Habitat for Humanity as "solution" or "failure," by political inclination of newspaper

	New York Times	*Toronto Star*	"LIBERAL" SUBTOTAL	*National/ Financial Post*	*Wall Street Journal*	*Washington Times*	"CONSERVATIVE" SUBTOTAL	TOTAL
TOTAL ARTICLES	432	412	844	81	104	264	449	1293
SUBSTANTIVE REFERENCES	130	197	327	24	39	86	149	476
HABITAT AS "SOLUTION" TO "GOVERNMENT FAILURE"	12	30	42	1	9	15	25	67
HABITAT AS INFERIOR TO GOVERNMENT	11	7	18	0	1	1	2	20

A few important findings are immediately evident. First, a large majority of articles were not classified as challenges to either interventionist government or the Habitat model. It should be repeated, though, that this is only because the coding scheme used here was cautious in that it omitted references that merely *implied* that Habitat was a better model. It only included articles in which Habitat was directly framed as superior, so the actual number of articles that highlighted "government failure" was higher than these numbers suggest. Nevertheless, the numbers do provide a useful foundation for comparing differences between the papers. Second, the *Toronto Star* seemed to have a distorting effect on the category of "liberal" in that it was significantly more likely than either its "liberal" U.S. counterpart, the *New York Times*, or the rest of the sample to frame Habitat as a positive alternative to "government failure." Third, the *National Post* was least frequently guilty of featuring Habitat as either a "solution" for "government failure" or as a problem in its own right. Fourth, "conservative" papers almost never framed Habitat as inferior to interventionist government, though admittedly they were also not that frequently guilty of framing it as a "solution" to the failures of such government.

Table 4.6 displays the chi-square comparisons across the liberal/conservative divide. As a category, "liberal" newspapers are no less likely than their "conservative" counterparts to position Habitat as a solution to "government

TABLE 4.6 Chi-square statistics comparing framing of government provision vis-à-vis Habitat for Humanity provision, by political inclination of newspaper

	"LIBERAL" NEWSPAPERS	"CONSERVATIVE" NEWSPAPERS	TOTAL	CHI STATISTIC	LEVEL OF SIGNIFICANCE
A. Habitat as "solution" to "government failure" in "liberal" vs. "conservative" newspapers					
"Government failure"	42	25	67	1.3101	0.252368721
Other	285	124	409		
Total	327	149	476		
B. Habitat as "solution" to "government failure" in "liberal" vs. "conservative" newspapers omitting *Toronto Star*					
"Government failure"	12	25	37	3.4384	0.063698634
Other	118	124	242		
Total	130	149	279		
C. Habitat as "inferior" to government solutions in "liberal" vs. "conservative" newspapers					
"Inferior" Habitat	18	2	20	4.4057	0.035819225
Other	309	147	456		
Total	327	149	476		
D. Habitat as "inferior" to government solutions in "liberal" vs. "conservative" newspapers omitting *Toronto Star*					
"Inferior Habitat"	11	2	13	7.9210	0.004886519
Other	119	147	266		
Total	130	149	279		

failure" (4.6A). However, if the *Toronto Star*—which featured a disproportionate number of articles criticizing local government vis-à-vis Habitat—is omitted, the story changes somewhat (4.6B). In this scenario, the remaining "liberal" newspaper (*New York Times*) was less likely (at the .10 level of significance) to position Habitat as a "solution" to "government failure" than the "conservative" newspapers as a whole. Turning the analysis to the frequency of framing Habitat as "inferior" to government-based housing solutions yielded a more definitive difference (4.6C and 4.6D). Liberal newspapers, whether or not the *Toronto Star* was included, were significantly more likely to position Habitat as inferior to government as a provider of housing. With the *Toronto Star* included under "liberal," the difference was significant at the .05 level of significance. Without the *Star*, the difference was significant at the .001 level.

In short, three findings emerge. First, the *Toronto Star* is an outlier among "liberal" newspapers. It is more likely than its "liberal" U.S. counterpart, the *New York Times*, or even the other conservative papers, to frame Habitat as a "solution" to "government failure." Second, liberal newspapers, with or without the *Toronto Star*, are significantly more likely to feature articles highlighting the limitations of Habitat vis-à-vis interventionist government. Quantitatively, the tendency to cast Habitat as a "solution" to "government failure" is only marginally more common in "conservative" newspapers than in "liberal" ones. Third, there are no statistical differences on the dimension of how Habitat is framed religiously (or not). Religious designations such as "an ecumenical organization" were sprinkled throughout the sample, as were nonspecific or secular descriptors, but the common thread in all was a casual usage of Habitat as an alternative to failed government. Not all were implicitly religious references, but many were implicitly or explicitly neoliberal.

Chi-square was also used to determine the extent to which differences in national context contributed to variation in positioning or description of Habitat. Why might such differences be expected? First, both Canada and the United States have experienced an aggressive turn away from publicly subsidized housing and toward nonprofit housing in the last thirty years, but this process began in the 1970s in the United States (Hackworth 2003), while it was not fully under way until the 1990s in Canada (Hackworth and Moriah 2006). In a sense, the differential existence of Habitat in the two countries speaks to this fact. Habitat as a model rose to prominence beginning in the late 1970s in the United States but not until the early 1990s in Canada. Second, while the actual ratio of publicly subsidized housing is not that different between the two countries—both around 5 percent depending on what is counted (Schwartz 2006; Hackworth 2008)—there is much less public antipathy to government intervention in sectors like housing in Canada than there is in the United States. Thus one might expect less criticism of government and more skepticism regarding the Habitat model in Canada. A chi-square analysis was performed to consider the extent to which these assumptions are accurate (see Hackworth 2009b for a more complete description of this).

Overall, expectations of a marked difference between countries in the coverage of Habitat were largely unjustified. Though there were significantly more "substantive" references to Habitat for Humanity in Canada — probably a reflection of the fact that its Canadian rise has been steeper and more recent — the differences between the countries in terms of religiosity and government positioning were mild. If the *Toronto Star* is included, Canadian papers were significantly more likely to characterize Habitat as a secular organization. If it is excluded, the differences evaporate, at least quantitatively. This does, however, belie important differences not revealed in the numbers. First, in recent years the *Toronto Star* (and to a lesser extent the *Globe and Mail*) was notably more inclined to refer to Habitat as a secular organization, just as it was becoming a more important provider of housing in Canada. Most characterizations in the United States, by contrast, fluctuated based on the context of the articles. When there was a need to emphasize religiosity — for example, during public discussions surrounding President Bush's Faith-Based Initiative — religiosity was highlighted (particularly in the *Washington Times* and the *Wall Street Journal*). When it seemed appropriate to emphasize the secular dimensions, this was the direction taken by the articles. In Canada, by contrast, there seemed to be a notable pattern of emphasizing either the secular aspects of Habitat for Humanity or avoiding any descriptors at all, particularly in more-recent articles. This tendency could be attributed to the fact that Canada has not thus far had a widespread faith-based welfare debate — and thus perhaps does not have the same need to discuss this dimension.

Differences on the dimension of "government failure" were even milder. There was no statistical difference between Canada and the United States in the frequency of articles that framed Habitat as a solution to "government failure." But this too overstates the similarities and belies the subtler political differences in the public cultures of the two countries that can be found beneath the numbers. First, there is no Canadian equivalent to the *Wall Street Journal* or the *Washington Times*. The "conservative" *National Post* was mostly noteworthy in its indifference to Habitat coverage. There were no blistering editorials about privatizing the welfare state using Habitat for Humanity as a vehicle in the *National Post*; there were several in each of its American counterparts. Second, the qualitative positioning of Habitat as either a problem or a solution differed between papers in the two countries. The *Toronto Star* was much more likely to emphasize ways in which Habitat was a solution to a failed local managerialist state but featured no broad-sweeping ideological editorials about privatizing the welfare state. It could be, in other words, that geography matters, but not as much as political inclinations and spatial differences in coverage (i.e., local versus national coverage).

RELIGIOUS NEOLIBERALISM AS COMMON SENSE

Very few people are acolytes of Gary North or profess to have a systematic religiously neoliberal worldview, but this does not mean that ideational fragments of this system of thought are wholly confined to the margins. In particular, the idea that governments are manifestly worse at providing welfare than organizations like Habitat for Humanity—despite evidence to the contrary—is widely held. This chapter has illustrated this phenomenon through an analysis of portrayals of Habitat for Humanity in a full spectrum of mainstream newspapers in the United States and Canada.

Habitat was framed as a replacement to government in at least three ways. First, openly ideological editorials and op-eds made this assertion directly. Habitat's religious elements and its independence from taxpayer funds were cited commonly as reasons for its value. Second, the organization was more subtly framed as overcoming one or more of the commonly accepted criticisms of government programs in North America. Habitat was portrayed as "a hand up, not a handout" that "rescued" people from publicly subsidized housing. Finally, local regulations were routinely framed as impediments to the operation of Habitat for Humanity. The idea that local governments impeded the organization with building codes served to further juxtapose the state and Habitat in these articles. The framing of Habitat as a solution to government failure is growing, widespread, and more or less consistent across the political spectrum of newspapers.

But the question remains: how much of the veneration of Habitat is associated with its religious roots, and how much is simply a by-product of being a widely known NGO—easy to use in articles because people are so familiar with it? In truth, Habitat's reputation probably stems from both factors, at least depending on the source in which it is under discussion. But as the organization becomes more prominent in the daily media discourse—most recent references to it do not even provide a sentence explaining its origins—it is becoming more and more implausible that the references are accidental or partially informed. Perhaps Habitat's religious roots are irrelevant. Perhaps it is just a nice organization that helps people in need. This is undoubtedly part of the reason it is invoked so frequently. But it is also likely that Habitat offers some a politically feasible way to criticize the welfare state and its recipients without being mean spirited. Its religious roots provide a sort of theological cover for ideas that sound a great deal more callous when spoken in secular terms. "Work harder and you will pull yourself out of poverty" sounds considerably more compassionate when cast under the rubric of quasi-Calvinistic Jesus economics than when inspired by quasi-individualistic Milton Friedman economics. This, of course, does not mean that everyone who invokes (or volunteers for) Habitat for Humanity as an alternative to state-led housing generation is somehow a Friedman acolyte disingenuously cloaked in the language of Jesus economics. But it also does not mean that Habitat's religious roots or its frequent discursive usage as an alternative to "failed government" are incidental or accidental. These references may be complicated in origin, but they surely to some extent orbit a common idea: that the state has failed and that religious charities are a palatable "force for good greater than government." Is it true also that even when the references are completely innocent of political content (if that's possible), they nonetheless help create a context that nourishes religious neoliberalism?

CHAPTER FIVE

Practicing Religious Neoliberalism

"President George W. Bush has emphasized the importance of faith-based organizations," writes Marvin Olasky in his foreword to *Enacted Christianity*, "the best of which help to change lives, the worst of which merely enable the destitute to remain in misery. Tens of thousands of self-sacrificing men and women are at work in those rescue missions across the country that are among the best" (2000, 9). What exactly makes one faith-based organization an enabler of destitution and another a life changer? Clearly, Marvin Olasky, author of the Bush administration's language of "compassionate conservatism" and long-time political insider for the faith-based social-services movement, has an idea of what that distinction would be. To Olasky, faith-based social services only make sense politically and practically if they are free from government — free to make their own rules, free to distinguish between the deserving and the undeserving, free to turn away anyone who does not adhere to their belief system, and above all, free from the universalizing principles of the welfare state, which have, in Olasky's view, exacerbated poverty in the United States (Olasky 1992). To religious neoliberals like Olasky, the faith-based social-services movement has always been about returning the welfare sector to its proper place: the openly sectarian confines of religious providers. This goal was precisely what many critics of the movement and the Bush administration's efforts to institutionalize it feared, namely, that welfare was simply the leading edge of a theocratically inspired takeover of the American state.[1]

But while the hyperbole of both sides of this debate has been, and remains, impressive, the literature — and there is a substantial amount of it — that tries to capture the actualized landscape of religious and nonreligious social service providers has generally yielded a more complicated picture than the fantasies of religious neoliberals or the fears of critics would imply. Most authors who have studied the faith-based social-service landscape before, during, and after the Bush administration have found a highly interconnected and variegated mix of providers. Even the most ostensibly antistatist organizations have indirect or direct contact or cooperation with some level of government, and even the most connected state-friendly FBOs engage in activities that make them more than a mere extension of the state.

This pervasive hybridization leaves researching actualized examples of religious neoliberalism highly challenging. No ideal-type organizations exist, so it is difficult to seriously evaluate the hopes of proponents or the fears of opponents. But the fact remains that religious neoliberals have publicly venerated certain types of existing FBOs, and it is worth considering those organizations in a book of this sort if only to explore the features that seem to appeal most to these advocates. This chapter explores what is arguably the most clear-cut form of religiously neoliberal welfare: the gospel rescue mission. Almost every city in the United States has one (many have more than one), and they are venerated by religious neoliberals largely because they shun government money and oversight, because they are openly sectarian, and because they emphasize personal responsibility far more assertively than their secular or government counterparts.

FINDING FAITH(-BASED ORGANIZATIONS)

The FBO literature has been rapidly expanding and multidisciplinary for the past ten years. The tone and nuance of this literature stand in marked contrast to the highly ideological and hyperbolic characterization of FBOs by figures like Olasky. If an archetypal FBO has emerged from this literature — and I am not convinced that it has — it is a pragmatic group, strapped for cash, doing its best to maintain its theological identity while chasing grants and donations from government, individuals, and foundations. The heroic FBO as replacement that Olasky pines for — one that resists the temptation of government funds and practices a tough-love Calvinism toward its clients — is rare (and possibly nonexistent) in practice and in the literature. But still, given the fears of opponents of the Faith-Based Initiative, it is intriguing that more effort has not been made to scrutinize those organizations that embody the ideals of religious neoliberalism.

Many studies of religious nonprofits focus primarily or exclusively on those that already receive government money. To receive government funds (especially, but not exclusively, federal funds), organizations secular and sectarian alike must abide by a set of regulations that prohibit (or discourage) them from using the resources to proselytize and from discriminating in whom they choose to serve (or hire). Given the dependency that many organizations have on government funds, the inclination is to abide by such regulations. Conversely, the very organizations most likely to be openly sectarian — faith saturated — are the ones least likely to apply for government funding (Ebaugh, Chafetz, and Pipes 2006).[2] Comparatively little research has been done on these organizations, namely, those that explicitly eschew government money so that they can maintain their religious bent. This is unfortunate, as these are precisely the organizations that have been the source of public controversy. One challenge, however, rests in finding such organizations. Homeless shelters notwithstanding, openly or pervasively sectarian organizations are rare in capital-intensive sectors like housing, as a relatively permanent (and lucrative) funding source (like government) is crucial to their survival (Goldsmith, Eimicke, and Torres 2006; Briggs 2004). Failure to comply with government regulations that explicitly prohibit certain hiring practices and the mixture of faith and service delivery would jeopardize their existence or at least their funding source.

Homeless shelters appear to be an exception, as many are affiliated in some way with a religious institution, and many are able to operate without consistent streams of government funding. In perhaps the most comprehensive study of its sort, the Urban Institute estimated that only 14 percent of homeless agencies (shelters, food programs, and advocacy programs) are government run, while 51 percent are run by secular nonprofits and 34 percent by religious nonprofits in the United States (Burt et al. 1999). Among religious nonprofits involved in homeless services, the Urban Institute determined that only 38 percent receive government funds and only 10 percent receive more than half of their funds from government sources. This stands in contrast to secular nonprofits, more than 75 percent of which receive government money, and 60 percent of which rely on this source for more than half of their budget (Aron and Sharkey 2002). But this study and most others fail to distinguish between faith-related institutions — those that accept government money, comply with government regulations, and have often done so for decades — and "faith-saturated" institutions, which are openly sectarian and shun the government money that might "pollute" their mission. Gospel rescue missions are a sorely understudied example of faith-saturated service providers that exist in every major city in the United States and supply a substantial percentage of the care received by homeless people.

Though several descriptive, generally promotional books, pamphlets, and web resources have been produced about rescue missions in the last thirty years (e.g., Bonner 2002; AGRM 2008), very little attention has been given to missions within the academic world. Undoubtedly the most important exception to this is the work of sociologist Ronald Fagan during the 1980s and 1990s. From Fagan's work and the aforementioned descriptive material, it is possible to assemble a brief description of the gospel rescue mission movement in the

United States (Fagan 1986a, 1986b, 1987, 1998). Rescue missions are highly varied in terms of size, scope, funding arrangements, and clientele. There are currently 284 members of the Association of Gospel Rescue Missions (AGRM) in the United States, though Arthur Bonner (2002) has argued that many other unaffiliated missions (perhaps as many as 100) exist as well. Budgets range from zero (all expenses paid out of pocket by volunteers) to over $10 million, and staff sizes are similarly variable. Many, though not all, rescue missions provide a meal service and some shelter for the homeless; most require attendance at chapel in return for this service. Collectively, according to the AGRM's most recent estimate (2006), rescue missions account for over 41 million meals and over 15 million bed-nights for the homeless annually. This translates into a total of 42,453 rescue mission shelter beds — roughly 20 percent of all emergency shelter beds and roughly 10 percent of all shelter beds including transitional housing (which is not as common among rescue missions) in the United States.[3] Other services include prisoner counseling, addiction therapy, clothing provision, and job counseling. The recent AGRM (2006) survey of services provided boasts of over 9 million mission chapel attendees and nearly 4 million Bible-study attendees alongside their bed and meal statistics. All gospel rescue missions are Christian, and most are fundamentalist or evangelical in their orientation.[4]

It is, in part, for this reason that most rescue missions have historically refused even to consider soliciting or receiving direct government funding. This inclination was fully intact as of the late 1980s (Fagan 1987), but various moves by Congress, including the 1996 Charitable Choice provisions of the Welfare Reform Act, and the Bush administration's Faith-Based Initiative have loosened this intransigence somewhat. In the past ten years, some missions have shown greater willingness to accept indirect funding and to apply for grants through the Bush administration's Compassion Capital Fund, while a smaller number have even hired professionals to lobby the federal government for direct funding (*New York Times* 2007b). Many missions, nonetheless, remain skeptical of the limitations that conditions linked to government funding would place on their activities. While other types of religious providers have willingly found ways to separate their sectarian and secular pursuits — a key requirement for receiving federal funds — most rescue missions have resisted doing so and remain suspicious even after the sea change at the federal level during the last fifteen years (since Charitable Choice). Most rescue mission volunteers and staff fervently believe that religious salvation is the first step toward material salvation, and many make this (or at least the appearance of it) a requirement for receiving food or shelter.[5]

It is difficult to find systematic assessments of how welcome or successful this approach is. The assessments are often more polemical than analytical in tone. Some anecdotal evidence from critics suggests that many homeless people do not approve of the approach and view it as insulting that their problems are individualized rather than viewed as arising from wider or structural conditions. As Ronald Fagan (1987) states, "Most of the men (and women) on skid row appear to resent the mission approach. Missions are seen as a last resort when other more attractive and less restrictive options are not available." The source of this resentment was encapsulated more recently in a frank manner by Kevin Barbieux (2008), a currently homeless blogger in Nashville, Tennessee:

> Christianity generally, and the Bible specifically, are subjects in need of exploring because a great many people respond to homelessness through them. Can there be a more easily manipulated person, to a confession of faith, than one suffering the burdens of homelessness? Some Christians will declare that during such difficult times, Christianity is in most need. Yet others will declare that people become homeless through Divine intervention—a ruse by God to get wayward people's attention. I can't tell you how many times a chaplain at the rescue mission chapel service will declare to the coerced attendants, "It is no accident that you are here tonight." Sadly, the rescue mission staff does not allow dissenting views to be expressed, on this subject, or any other. . . . Although the rescue mission claims that it is non-denominational, only fundamentalist views are allowed to be expressed at the mission.

Not everyone shares this view, however. Interviews conducted for this chapter, for example, indicate that many of the homeless in New York City *prefer* rescue missions over government-run shelters because they are safer and quieter. And there are, of course, ardent supporters of the approach. Supporters are just as unambiguous in their thinking but obviously draw different conclusions. In his influential *Tragedy of American Compassion*, Religious Right leader Olasky (1992) identified rescue missions as the model upon which the welfare state should be rebuilt. Unfortunately, however, little has been done by less ideological scholars to interrogate the distinctions between rescue missions and government-provided welfare. Although there is an interesting descriptive literature on rescue missions and many are, by default, included in wider studies of profits (e.g., Twombly 2002), no explicit attempt has been made to study such organizations within the meso-context of the faith-based social services movement (see Fagan 1998 for a mild exception to this) or within the meta-context of neoliberalizing urbanization (Hackworth 2007). This study attempts to fill this void. The first step toward that end is to provide a general portrait of gospel rescue missions in the United States based on a web survey and a variety of secondary statistics.

SURVEYING THE LANDSCAPE OF RESCUE MISSIONS

Empirically, this chapter is based on material from two main sources: a web-based survey of gospel rescue missions, and more detailed, city-level profiles of rescue missions in three U.S. cities (New York, Phoenix, and Nashville). The web-based survey included all members of the Association of Gospel Rescue Missions (as indicated by their website).[6] A response rate of 37.7 percent (107 rescue missions) was achieved by sending out e-mail notices and a hyperlink to an online survey service (SurveyMonkey).[7] Questions in the survey revolved primarily around three themes: (1) basic features of the rescue mission; (2) perceived differences between the rescue mission's approach to service versus the approach of its secular counterparts; and (3) its relationship with, and views of, government funding and regulation. All the actual individual respondents were paid staff members of the rescue missions in question, and 82.2 percent (eighty-three) were directors or other management-level officials.

Table 5.1 displays the distribution in size and activities of the rescue missions that responded. As the table indicates, almost all (98.2 percent) of the respondents provided shelter services, and most were relatively large in size (e.g., over fifty beds). Meal services were even more widespread (100 percent of the respondents) and tended to be large in scale; most responding missions served over one hundred meals per day. Most had over ten employees and twenty volunteers in a given week. The average annual budget was over $1 million, and nearly 40 percent had budgets over $2 million. These funds were derived from a variety of sources (table 5.2), the most common being individual donations, corporate contributions, grants from foundations, bequests, and congregational giving.[8] The money was used to finance an array of services extending beyond meals and beds (table 5.3). Solid majorities provided job-skills training (74.5 percent) and drug-use support programs (66.7 percent), while notable percentages provided youth programs (25.5 percent), a prison ministry (26.5 percent), a medical clinic (45.1 percent), and community outreach (42.2 percent). Almost all the respondent organizations (96.1 percent) also provided regular chapel services, and 66 percent required attendance for some or all of their clientele. As table 5.4 indicates, however, some missions imposed this rule more rigidly than others. Some positioned it directly as a requirement before a person could receive a meal or shelter, while others were quick to point out that it was required, or just suggested, to obtain only some services. Others,

TABLE 5.1 Basic characteristics of rescue mission respondents to survey

ANSWER OPTIONS	RESPONSE PERCENT	RESPONSE COUNT*
Number of people sheltered on an average night		
Under 10	2.9	3
11–50	19.0	20
51–100	32.4	34
101–500	41.0	43
Over 500	2.9	3
No shelter services provided	1.9	2
Meals served in an average day		
Under 10	0.0	0
11–50	5.7	6
51–100	9.5	10
101–500	64.8	68
Over 500	20.0	21
No meal services provided	0	0
Number of regular employees		
Under 5	8.6	9
6–10	16.2	17
11–20	20.0	21
21–50	31.4	33
Over 50	23.8	25
Volunteers in a typical week		
Under 5	2.9	3
6–10	14.4	15
11–20	23.1	24
21–50	26.0	27
Over 50	33.7	35
Annual operating budget		
Under $200,000	5.8	6
$200,001–$500,000	19.2	20
$500,001–$1,000,000	19.2	20
$1,000,001–$2,000,000	14.4	15
Over $2,000,000	40.4	42
Unsure	1.0	1

*Not all counts add up to 105 because not all questions were answered by all respondents.

TABLE 5.2 Sources of revenue for rescue mission respondents

ANSWER OPTIONS	RESPONSE PERCENT	RESPONSE COUNT
Individual donations	99.0	104
Corporate/business giving	86.7	91
Foundation giving	82.9	87
Special fund-raising events	73.3	77
Bequests	71.4	75
Religious denomination funding (local, regional, or national)	61.9	65
Secular nonprofit organizations (e.g., the United Way)	48.6	51
Endowment or investment income	46.7	49
Dues, fees, and charges for services	36.2	38
Other religious federated organizations (e.g., Catholic Charities)	26.7	28
Sales of products (e.g., literature)	29.5	31
Other	29.5	31
Government-sector third-party payments (e.g., Medicare or Medicaid)	10.5	11

Note: respondents were permitted to select more than one option.

perhaps sensing that such a policy seems severe, were quick to note that the requirement was not as onerous as it sounded. One respondent offered the qualification: "Attendance is required, but participation is not."

Most missions reported that their services were in high demand and that demand had increased over the recent short and medium term. The AGRM does periodic surveys of the entirety of rescue missions, and results generally corroborate this perception of recent growth (AGRM 2008). Its figures show that the number of rescue mission bed-nights in the United States increased 71 percent (5.9 percent per year) between 1994 and 2006; from 9,055,000 in

TABLE 5.3 Services provided by rescue mission respondents

ANSWER OPTIONS	RESPONSE PERCENT	REPONSE COUNT
Prepared meals served	98.1	102
Chapel services	96.2	100
Job-skills training program	74.8	77
Drug-use support group	66.0	68
Development department staff	64.1	66
Community food pantry	46.2	48
Medical clinic	45.6	47
Community outreach	41.7	43
Other	38.8	40
Facilities for abused women	35.0	36
Jail and prison ministry	26.2	27
Youth programs	25.2	26
Child care program	22.3	23
Residential program for mentally ill	14.6	15
Legal clinic	13.6	14
Drop-in center for mentally ill	8.7	9
Special program for senior citizens	8.7	9
English as a second language	4.9	5

Note: respondents were permitted to select more than one option.

1994, to 13,713,817 in 2003, to 15,495,197 in 2006. Meals served per day also increased during this time period from 27,400,000 in 1994, to 35,577,139 in 2003, to 41,885,652 in 2006. Directly comparable statistics for other homeless shelters in the United States are difficult to obtain, but several recent studies indicate an overall growth in the number of shelter beds lower than the rescue mission rate. The U.S. Conference of Mayors (2007), for example, found a 4.9 percent increase in all shelter beds and a 2.8 percent increase in emergency shelter beds

TABLE 5.4 Selected responses to the question "Is chapel attendance mandatory?"

COMMENTS PROVIDED IN THE "PLEASE ELABORATE" BOX TO CHAPEL QUESTION
Mandatory for all residents staying in shelter. However, clients coming in for food, furniture, and/or household items are not required to go to any services.
Strongly suggested for shelter guests but not officially required for any. Chapel is a part of our long term aftercare program, and residents are expected to be a part of that.
Individuals who wish to spend the night at our mission MUST attend the chapel service.
Not required in order to receive food or other benefits, but it is required of those who are residents of the mission.
For the men in our program chapel services are mandatory. However, for our Senior Care or for those who come in off the street to have a meal, it is suggested that they participate in chapel before a meal.
When people come to the mission, they know they are going to get a good meal, a clean and safe place to sleep, and a gospel message as well. For we are not ashamed of the gospel, for it is the power of God unto salvation, for everyone that believes (Romans 1:16). We believe it is the power of God that transforms lives through the Word of God. Therefore, why would we not share it? It is sin in people's lives that harden their heart, not hearing the gospel.
Anyone is free to not attend services; however, we have not experienced anyone not wanting to attend.
Evening or morning chapel/devotions can be missed if employment conflicts, but both cannot be missed in a single day.
Chapel is mandatory for shelter guests for the first 30 days then only Sunday and Wednesday required. Suggested for children in care but not required.
It is mandatory for our overnight guests but being alert/awake isn't mandatory.
Attendance required. Participation is not.

(the variable most comparable to most rescue missions) in its 2007 survey of twenty-three large American cities. These data compare to a 7.8 percent increase in rescue mission beds during a similar period, between 2005 and 2006 (AGRM 2008).

Although rescue missions shared an increase in demand for services with their secular counterparts, many respondents were quick to distinguish their brand of services from government programs, secular nonprofits, and faith-related organizations. While over 66 percent of respondents felt that there was no fundamental difference between their clientele and those who sought out secular and government-run shelters, many offered comments hinting at a different set of expectations for their clients (table 5.5). Many of the answers clearly indicated that while the people themselves might not have been different, the programs and expectations were. Others were less restrained in distinguishing the people themselves. Further hints at differences between missions and other shelters were revealed when respondents were asked about access. Only 41.4 percent felt that there were differences (11.1 indicated they "did not know"), but the open-ended responses tell a more detailed story (table 5.6). Some focused on how it was logistically easier (or more difficult) to gain access to their facility, while others suggested that an admission of personal failure was a necessary precondition for gaining access. When asked to elaborate more generally in an open-ended fashion about the differences between their services and those provided by the government, even more respondents (sixty three) offered their view, and most were quick to make distinctions (table 5.7). Most responses to this question focused on the role of "faith," "compassion," and "redemption" in the services they provided (versus government). Others pointed out that they were the only facility in their city. Still others emphasized that they dealt with the root of the problem, which varied from an individual's unwillingness to accept Christ to his unwillingness to admit alcoholism.

Over 60 percent of respondents indicated that they refused to receive or pursue government funding of any sort. This figure is somewhat lower than that in the AGRM's (2008) 1994 study, which shows that 69 percent of missions did not take government funds. For those that did receive government funds and were willing to specify, the sources of support were highly varied. At the federal level, HUD (U.S. Department of Housing and Urban Development), FEMA (Federal Emergency Management Agency), and the USDA (U.S. Department of Agriculture) were common sources. Community Development Block Grants (CDBG), McKinney Act funds, Emergency Shelter grants, and Community Action grants were mentioned frequently. At the state level, various housing, social service, and redevelopment agencies were cited. At the local level, most support was referred to nonspecifically as from "the city" or "the county," but several missions did specify that they had a formally contracted relationship with their city to provide beds or food for the homeless. In several cases, missions specified that they received only money that came without restrictions placed on their sectarian efforts. But overall, the majority of missions proudly proclaimed their independence from government. Though 81.8 percent of the

TABLE 5.5 Selected responses to the question "What are the differences between the clientele who seek out your services and those that seek out government-provided ones?"

ON WHY HOMELESS PERSONS CHOOSE THEIR ORGANIZATION OVER GOVERNMENT-PROVIDED SERVICES . . .
Most of our clientele are looking for a biblically based organization.
Those coming to us are interested in life change, not just receiving a meal and/or a bed.
Many consider us to be their church.
To some degree—there are clients who come here because we are a Christian shelter and program and they desire that environment. Others don't care and are just seeking a place to stay.
Because we are a nondenominational Christ-centered mission, men seeking a change in their lives may see our programs and services as a better choice than a government or secular service. We have a reputation for being a safe, comfortable place to stay.
They are the same clients. The shelter that is close to our facility is merely a day shelter, so those who need overnight shelter come to our facility. We have a good relationship with the other service-provider.
They are more committed to life change and willing to abstain from the use of alcohol and drugs.
For some, the mission is considered safer. The emphasis on a spiritual connection with God and Jesus has appeal for others.
More religious oriented and possibly more motivated to change.
From our surveys, most who come to us prefer a faith-based place to stay. They feel safe here and appreciate the hope given.
Many of our clients are looking for a Christian facility.
Because most of the time they are the same people. For instance, our women and children's shelter is always full, and so we rely on the other organizations to house them until we have an opening. We work well with all of the other organizations in our community.
They want the bread of LIFE!
Many of our clients are those who have cycled through other shelters and other programs and yet are still homeless. When they despair of "emergency shelter" programs, when they have exhausted all other resources, and when they have reached a point where they desire life change from the inside out, the homeless often turn to the rescue mission.

TABLE 5.6 Selected responses to the question "What are the differences between access requirements for clients seeking out your services versus those for government-provided ones?"

ON DIFFERENCES IN ACCESS REQUIREMENTS FOR CLIENTELE . . .
City restrictions will not allow us to shelter men previously released from prison who are still on parole. Also we are not allowed to shelter anyone with a criminal sexual conduct conviction.
Attend religious services.
We serve many people that the other shelters cannot serve (i.e., those who have certain criminal backgrounds).
We screen clients for financial information, willingness to work, etc.
They only need a picture ID to check in to our facility.
Maybe just the above that they choose to be drug free . . .
Varies with the service. No one is denied access on religious grounds, but we do require involvement in religious activities for those in our residential recovery programs.
Almost all other shelters require a referral. We take all regardless of being referred or just walking in off the street.
Desire for positive change.
Accessing our services is actually a bit more user-friendly than most other facilities.
The client must shed all external support structures upon entering the program, including welfare. Clients cannot have a car or a cell phone; they must adhere to the no alcohol/drugs requirement.
We look for men who can freely state that their life is out of control and that without help, they are on the road to physical death. Most men who come to us have been through four previous programs and failed or left prior to completion.
We do not provide services for illegal aliens.
We take everyone as long as they are not under the influence of drugs or alcohol and they are tested if suspicion is evident, and Breathalyzer [is required] for every client.

respondents reported having had no major conflict with government over the nature of their outreach, most (79 percent) also believed that such an alliance would restrict their ability to "preach the gospel" to their clients. Said one respondent representative of this perspective, "We never want to be in a position where we cannot share the gospel of Jesus Christ. Our concern is that procedures or regulations may change and then we are reliant on such funding. We do not want to rely on the government for our funding." Much smaller percentages of respondents reported not seeking government funding because the application procedures were too onerous (19.8 percent) or because their organizations were completely self-sufficient with other sources of income (28.4 percent). The majority simply felt that their efforts would be restricted by government and that any material benefit would be outweighed by such restrictions. Strangely, given the significant effort by the Bush administration and the apparent continuation of some of these policies by the Obama administration, rescue missions generally felt more welcomed at the local than the federal level. When asked to assess whether they felt that the political atmosphere at the city level was becoming more or less receptive toward services like theirs, only 14.3 percent felt that it was "less," with the rest indicating either that it was more receptive or that they did not know. Respondents were notably less sanguine when asked the same question about the political atmosphere in the United States more generally. When asked about the influence of recent specific initiatives at the federal level — Charitable Choice, the Faith-Based Initiative, and the Compassion Capital Fund — the majority of respondents suggested that these programs increased neither their ability nor their willingness to apply for government funds. Perhaps most disappointing for prosectarian government policy makers may be the findings regarding the Compassion Capital Fund — a program set up explicitly to bring previously marginalized organizations (like rescue missions) into the social service fold by increasing their capacity to apply successfully for grants. Almost 71 percent said that the Compassion Capital Fund did not affect their ability to apply for government funds, and 66.8 percent said that it did not even affect their willingness to do so. Table 5.8 displays some of the open-ended responses to this line of questioning; the level of skepticism is notable. Though some were grateful for the Bush administration's efforts (and blamed Congress for changing the Faith-Based Initiative), many felt that they, along with the rest of the evangelical community, were being politically manipulated (cf. Kuo 2006) by the initiatives. Said one frustrated official, "Faith-Based Initiatives are a joke. It was a political tool to engage evangelicals to vote for the Bush administration. I do not doubt President Bush's personal concern for the poor, but the program is evidence that it is and was low priority." Many rescue missions remained skeptical of federal government efforts even if they were being prosecuted by a putative ally in the Bush administration and the Obama administration has not meaningfully overturned them. Most respondents were more trustful of their municipality, county, or state than they were of the federal government efforts, no matter how supportive the White House professes to be.

TABLE 5.7 Selected responses to the question "What are the general differences between your services and comparable ones offered by the government in your city?"

ON GENERAL DIFFERENCES . . .
We feel that there generally is not a life change until there is a heart change. Our goal is to help our residents find a life change from that of a homeless lifestyle to one of independence through a relationship with God.
We operate from a Christian perspective.
We provide the opportunity (voluntary) to see and hear the message of Jesus Christ. We want them to know we love them and hope for them. We will walk with them through the ups and downs challenging them to know God and also to improve their situation.
Spiritual component missing from the secular places. The whole person is not dealt with in the secular area.
We offer long-term, effective solutions to homelessness, as opposed to simply providing shelter.
There are no other services for homeless in our area.
We offer optional spiritual services that government services don't. Often, program members heal more quickly with a spiritual grounding, and spiritual resources at their disposal advance that process.
Much more effective with a success rate of more than 84% — the foundation of relation with God through Jesus Christ is key in our success rate.
There aren't any government-run shelters here.
We offer a spiritual component that gives clients the opportunity to find purpose, hope, forgiveness, and God's grace.
We provide a spiritual element to our services that allow a person to examine themselves and receive spiritual direction. Decisions are biblically based.

In short, rescue missions provide a form of social service for highly marginalized populations that is self-consciously distinctive from government-provided aid, faith-related aid, and secular nonprofit aid. This form of service emphasizes individual and spiritual causes for poverty and demands repentance by its clientele. Many respondents to the survey conducted for this study perceived an increase in demand for their organizations' services over the past decade, a perception supported by nationwide shelter bed counts. These fig-

TABLE 5.7 ***(continued)***

ON GENERAL DIFFERENCES . . .
I believe our staff is more compassionate and has an interest in the individual that goes beyond providing the basics of life, i.e., food, shelter, etc.
WE BELIEVE THAT A PERSONAL RELATIONSHIP TO JESUS CHRIST IS FOUNDATIONAL FOR THE HEALING OF A PERSON'S BODY, MIND AND SPIRIT. THIS IN TURN LEADS TO A COMPLETELY DIFFERENT OUTLOOK ON LIFE THAT CHANGES THEM AND THEIR WORLD. (emphasis in original)
The program is based on understanding and changing from the inside, not making outward changes. Until the heart changes, the actions usually do not change over time. Better food, a more compassionate approach in which we treat each client with a high level of dignity and respect; we offer the critical element of hope in addition to basic services such as food, shelter, and clothing.
Government services are designed to only meet emergency food, clothing, and shelter needs. Our programs are designed to meet emergency needs and to prepare the person to resolve issues and to provide for themselves through traditional means.
We are a Christ-based organization, and so we try to get to the root of a client's problem. We don't want to just put a band aid on it and send them on their way. We look to make each person who comes to the mission a productive citizen in society again.
We deal more with the heart of the problem that just providing a band aid to the problem. The obvious, ours is ministry based and, in my opinion, more effective.
I believe our overnight shelter is safer because we lock up all of our guests' personal items, and they do not have access to it. The secular shelter down the street cannot require personal items to be locked up. Therefore, there people are concerned with getting things stolen, drugs or alcohol being used, or access to weapons etc. This policy makes the overnight shelter safer for our guests as well as our employees.
Jesus is lifted up.

ures also suggest that rescue missions are growing at a faster rate than the rest of the shelter world. But while missions seem to be becoming a more central part of the homeless-shelter universe, their skepticism toward government aid, particularly federal government support, seems to be intact. Most respondents reported a refusal to take direct government aid, fearful that it would inhibit their brand of service delivery. Many fewer felt that governmental authorities in their locality would inhibit them similarly.

TABLE 5.8 Selected responses to the question "What influence have recent federal programs had on your organization's stance toward government funding?"

ON RECENT FEDERAL PROGRAMS . . .
For over 115 years we have had no interest nor need for government funding and its accompanying programmatic interference. There is no evidence or reason, now or in the future, to change our position.
We are a conservative gospel rescue mission. We do not and will not take government funding.
We have just been told we are not eligible for any state or federal funding because of our chapel service being mandatory plus the new Housing First Program's goal is to eliminate shelters altogether so what is the sense of even trying to apply.
We will not compromise our mission to share the love of Christ with others, so I guess we will just have to depend on God for our survival and not our government.
A more positive atmosphere was created by these initiatives and less of a bias was noticed.
Faith Based Initiatives are a joke. It was a political tool to engage evangelicals to vote for the Bush administration. I do not doubt President Bush's personal concern for the poor, but the program is evidence that it is and was low priority. Read David Kuo's book *Tempting Faith* and you will get a better understanding of what I'm referring to. I thought you said this would take just 10 minutes? Anyway, thanks for what you do and I hope this helps in some small way.
We appreciate what President Bush is doing in his Faith-Based Initiative programs. However, at this point, we still choose to be autonomous.
We have had all the funding necessary to carry out the work the Lord has called us to do. To look to the government after 54 years of service would suggest that God is not able to meet our needs. Also with the political change in D.C. one year it might be favorable and the next with different leadership the winds of change will happen. We choose not to become dependent on the government for our support.

RESCUE MISSIONS IN NEW YORK, PHOENIX, AND NASHVILLE

The survey was useful for collecting information at the national level, but it is also important to understand how the experiences of gospel missions as a group vary between cities. So profiles of geographical variation in the role of the rescue missions within the context of their specific local social safety net were also conducted for this chapter. The profiles draw upon more-intensive interviews with rescue mission personnel and public officials in each city, local and national reports on homelessness, and information obtained from each

TABLE 5.8 (*continued*)

ON RECENT FEDERAL PROGRAMS . . .
We feel that government funds are not sustainable and are subject to challenge for activities that may appear to be patently religious in the future even if they are determined to be neutral currently.
After legislatures revised President Bush's "faith-based initiatives," it became illegal for nonprofits of faith-based organizations to proselytize without giving them the option not be proselytized. This is the very purpose of our organization, for almost 100 years, to proselytize Jesus Christ. Why then would we take funding and then allow people not to hear the message? We often have people come to the mission who do not want to hear a message. However, it is the very power of God that transforms or changes their lives. Why then would we make this optional? Faith-based initiatives are good for organizations that are not completely faith based or are willing to compromise how they provide services.
We are skeptical of the faith-based initiatives because we do not know if or when they could be changed and we would no longer be able to depend upon them.
This relaxing of restrictions has made it possible for state and local agencies to feel free to give to those organizations that are doing the job and yet are religious. We feel free with them also.
I believe that when it first came out, the director thought that we would be able to get federal funds to hire someone as a grant writer. That never materialized and she had to find another job. I think after that there was some fear as to how receiving any faith-based funds would limit our ability to share the gospel.
Our primary mission is to preach the gospel of Jesus Christ through the work of rescue ministry. Receiving any kind of federal monies allows the government to dictate how and when you are allowed to minister the gospel.

rescue mission's website. The overarching goal was to detect variation in the role of each rescue mission within the broader context of the particular social safety net in which it is embedded. The descriptions below are intended to be not comprehensive case studies of the mission approach to homelessness in each city but rather small profiles of the rescue missions in each city to emphasize the basic geographical variation in the role that each plays. The aim was to select three places with different political histories vis-à-vis the Keynesian welfare state. Three cities — New York, Phoenix, and Nashville — were chosen as extremes along this continuum. New York has long had one of the most substantial safety nets for homeless persons in the United States. Phoenix, by contrast, has a history of secular antigovernmentalism that has led to a rather thin safety net that nonprofits are relied upon to supplement. Nashville is a smaller city that has had a noted influence of religion in general, and religious welfare in particular, compared to New York or Phoenix. The differential experience of gospel rescue missions in these three cities parallels the uneven landscape of religious neoliberalism in the United States more broadly.

New York City

Though it has suffered decades of decline and is the virtually constant target of conservatives (Peck 2006a), New York City had, and continues to have, one of the most extensive municipal welfare systems in the United States. It has, for example, the best public housing system in the country and until recently had more generous aid allotments than other cities in the United States. Its regulations regarding homeless people are dictated in large part by three New York State Supreme Court cases from the 1980s. In the first of these cases, *Callahan v. Carey*, the New York–based Coalition for the Homeless filed suit on behalf of three homeless men who were seeking shelter in the city's Bowery neighborhood (Coalition for the Homeless n.d.). The case lasted several years, until 1981, when it was settled by a consent decree. Based on their reading of the New York State Constitution, the court upheld the coalition's position that homeless men were entitled to the right to shelter in New York. In 1983, this right was extended to women as a result of the *Eldredge v. Koch* case and to families with children as a result of the subsequent *McCain v. Koch* case. The city was ordered to provide accommodation to all those seeking it after this point. To meet this need, the city manages the largest shelter system in the country and also relies heavily on nonprofits, secular and sectarian (including three rescue missions). Of course, this does not mean that the regulations have been applied evenly since being decreed by the court. Mayor Rudy Giuliani (1994–2001) was famously more restrictive in defining "homeless" than his predecessor, Mayor David Dinkins (1990–93), or his successor, Mayor Michael Bloomberg (*New York Times* 2007b).

The city does provide referrals to rescue missions but does not (as far as I could discern) favor them over its other referral organizations. According to HUD's most recent figures, the shelter population of New York City's "Continuum of Care" (CoC) was 46,617 in 2007.[9] There are 264 rescue mission shelter beds in New York, serving roughly 0.56 percent of the total sheltered population (table 5.9).[10] There are four rescue missions in New York City: the New York City Rescue Mission, the Bowery Mission, Saint Paul's House in Manhattan, and the much newer Brooklyn Rescue Mission (table 5.10). The

TABLE 5.9 Selected comparison of shelter statistics in New York, Phoenix, and Nashville

CITY	CITY POPULATION*	METROPOLITAN AREA POPULATION†	2007 SHELTERED HOMELESS POPULATION‡	CHANGE FROM 2006	2007 UNSHELTERED HOMELESS POPULATION	CHANGE FROM 2006	RESCUE MISSION BEDS	PERCENT OF HOMELESS SHELTER COUNT
New York	8,143,197	18,747,320	46,617	-9.8%	3,755	-2.3%	264	.56%
Phoenix	1,461,575	3,865,077	5,595	+3.3%	2,853	+38.3%	90	1.6%
Nashville	549,110	1,422,544	1,766	+18.8%	390	-21.4%	638	36.1%

Sources: HUD 2008; U.S. Census 2008; U.S. Census 2006.

* Population statistics are derived from the *City and County Databook* (a U.S. Census publication) and based on 2005 counts.

† Metropolitan area statistics are derived from the *State and Metropolitan Area Data Book* (a U.S. Census publication) and based on 2005 counts.

‡ Sheltered and unsheltered population estimates are derived from the Department of Housing and Urban Development's most recent report to Congress on homelessness (2008). The estimates reported here are only for the Continuum of Care geographic designation for the city in question. New York's CoC is the same as the geographic boundaries of the city; Phoenix's includes all of Maricopa County (and thus most of the metropolitan area), and Nashville's includes all of Davidson County (which contains about half of the metropolitan area). Unsheltered numbers are notoriously unreliable and almost certainly undercount the true total (not to mention missing entirely those who are functionally but not visibly homeless). These figures are used here only to make relative comparisons between the cities, not as a reliable count of the actual level of homelessness in each city.

New York City Rescue Mission — established as the Water Street Mission in 1872 — is the oldest continuously running rescue mission in the United States. It is located on Lafayette Street in Lower Manhattan and runs a variety of programs to help the chronically and periodically homeless, including a soup kitchen and an emergency shelter. According to interviews with staff and information from the mission's website, the facility contains 100 emergency beds for men and serves 334 meals per day. Chapel attendance is required for those wishing to use one of the beds but not for those arriving only for a meal. There are currently 23 staff members at the NYC Rescue Mission, and it operates with an annual budget of $4.7 million, approximately 4 percent of which is derived from government sources.

TABLE 5.10 Selected characteristics of rescue missions in New York City, Phoenix, and Nashville

NAME	DATE OF ESTABLISHMENT	APPROXIMATE OPERATING BUDGET	APPROXIMATE PERCENT OF BUDGET DERIVED FROM GOVERNMENT SOURCES	STAFF SIZE	TOTAL SHELTER BEDS	DAILY MEALS SERVED	SERVICES PROVIDED
NEW YORK CITY*							
NYC Rescue Mission	1872	$4.7 million	4	23	100	334	Chapel services, career counseling, food pantry, medical and vision care, family court, lunch, and drug counseling
Bowery Mission	1878	$9.2 million	Unknown	92	154	1,301	Chapel services, career counseling, food pantry, after-school program, summer camp, medical and vision care
Saint Paul's House	1945	$200,000	12.5	6	10	72	Chapel services, career counseling, food pantry, youth program, GED assistance

The Bowery Mission also has a long history (established 1878) and offers a variety of community services, but it is nearly twice the size of the NYC Rescue Mission. With a budget of $9.2 million, the Bowery Mission has several locations in Manhattan, including the original site (still located on the Bowery), the administrative headquarters and Women's Center on the Upper East Side, a transitional housing facility (also in Manhattan), and a retreat in Pennsylvania. It offers a variety of services including shelter and prepared food. According to interviews and the Bowery Mission website, the organization has a total of

TABLE 5.10 *(continued)*

NAME	DATE OF ESTABLISHMENT	APPROXIMATE OPERATING BUDGET	APPROXIMATE PERCENT OF BUDGET DERIVED FROM GOVERNMENT SOURCES	STAFF SIZE	TOTAL SHELTER BEDS	DAILY MEALS SERVED	SERVICES PROVIDED
PHOENIX							
Phoenix Rescue Mission	1952	$9.4 million	0	76	90	687	Chapel services, food pantry, career counseling, addiction recovery, family and community outreach, emergency shelter
NASHVILLE							
Nashville Rescue Mission	1953	$6.8 million	0	82	638	1,502	Chapel services, food pantry, career counseling, educational outreach, emergency shelter

Sources: Websites for each rescue mission and interviews with officials at each rescue mission.

* New York City technically has four rescue missions (those listed above plus the Brooklyn Rescue Mission). However, because the Brooklyn Rescue Mission does not run either a soup kitchen or a shelter, it was omitted from this table.

154 beds: 77 transitional housing beds, 60 emergency shelter beds at the original Bowery Mission, and 17 beds at the Women's Center. There are ninety-two regular staff members, and around seventy more people are hired during the summer, primarily to work at one of the organization's several summer camps for underprivileged youth. Interviewees were vague about whether chapel was a requirement for those using their services, but they did emphasize the importance of faith in the improvement of their clients' lives. Staff at the Bowery Mission were also unclear about the amount of government funding the or-

ganization receives but did not express a blanket aversion to it in principle and mentioned at least one program (the transitional housing program) that received direct governmental support.

Saint Paul's House, located in the Hell's Kitchen neighborhood of Manhattan, is much smaller and newer than the other two Manhattan missions. Founded in 1945, Saint Paul's House has an annual budget of $200,000, almost 90 percent of which comes from nongovernmental sources (primarily donations). Saint Paul's has six regular employees with about ten additional volunteers per day. It provides a more limited range of services than the two other Manhattan missions but has a notable emphasis on food preparation. In 2007, it prepared 26,247 meals (72 per day) and filled another 6,400 shopping bags with groceries. In addition to its small emergency shelter (ten beds), it also runs summer camps and offers GED training. An interview with a staff member revealed that Saint Paul's does not require chapel attendance for a meal. The staff member acknowledged that this was a "tricky" issue for the organization and noted that its philosophy was to separate its religious and social service activities as much as possible. The respondent also noted that Saint Paul's clientele had expressed a desire to stay at its facility in large part because they felt it was safer than government-run shelters. This contrasts with many of the survey respondents (in other cities) who focused on the religious inclination of their clientele as a chief reason for their desire to seek out the mission's services. Finally, the Brooklyn Rescue Mission is the newest (founded in 2002) and smallest of the four registered missions in New York. It does not have an emergency shelter or a soup kitchen but does provide food distribution programs. It is aligned openly with secular agencies like the United Way and focuses on urban agriculture and food security.

Overall, the history of rescue missions is the deepest in New York (compared to Phoenix and Nashville), but it is also the most enmeshed in the existing secular and government-funded safety net. Rescue mission managers were careful to distinguish their model of service and to emphasize the importance of personal responsibility and faith in God as necessary conditions for emerging from poverty, but the missions were also connected to secular organizations like the United Way and accepted some form of government funding without protest.

Phoenix

Phoenix, in contrast to New York, is a newer city whose political history has been more dismissive toward welfare and government regulation. It is the political base from which Barry Goldwater rose to prominence on an antigovernment platform in the 1960s. The population has increased in size considerably since then, and the political fault lines have become more complicated, but there are still strands of antigovernmentalism within the Phoenix welfare safety net. Like many cities in the Sun Belt, Phoenix has a great number of migrants, some of whom come for work and when unsuccessful find their way into the shelter system. Unlike other cities in the United States, where HUD recently found a decrease in the homeless population, Phoenix recorded an increase in both its sheltered and unsheltered homeless population, the latter growing an alarming 38.3 percent between 2006 and 2007 (table 5.9). Like most of HUD's homelessness counts, these figures are disputed strenuously (as being an underrepresentation of the true numbers) by local officials, who estimate the daily number of homeless people in the region at seven thousand to ten thousand (U.S. Conference of Mayors 2007). Phoenix does not maintain government-run shelters but does have a close relationship with the secular nonprofit Watkins Overflow Shelter in downtown Phoenix (U.S. Conference of Mayors 2007). Recent efforts have focused on preventing new entrants to the shelter system, a difficult task in a region so tied to the mortgage crisis, which has led to unemployment, eviction, and foreclosure increases well above the national rate. The city also provides a referral service for homeless services provided by nonprofits, many of which are faith related — one, the Phoenix Rescue Mission, is a faith-saturated operation. Officials estimate that, in total, the system of nonprofit shelters can handle only two-thirds of the homeless population in Phoenix's CoC (U.S. Conference of Mayors 2007).

The Phoenix Rescue Mission (PRM) is located just west of downtown and has a budget of $9.2 million (table 5.10). Founded in 1952, the mission provides a range of services including a chapel, a food pantry, career counseling, addiction recovery, family and community outreach, and an emergency shelter. The facility houses ninety men per night, or approximately 1.6 percent of the sheltered population in the Phoenix CoC. Like the other rescue mission officials interviewed for this study, officials at the PRM indicated that faith is the central element of their program that positively distinguishes it from secular nonprofits and government providers. Chapel attendance is required of those wishing to spend the night at the PRM, but not for those seeking one of its 687 daily meals. The PRM does not accept government money. Staff interviews indicated a fear that this might restrict its religious bent.

Overall, the faith-saturated safety net for Phoenix as it is expressed by its rescue mission does not constitute a large percentage of the web of options for homeless people. Though mission officials were not adamant, they were firmly against pursuing government funds, either federally or locally. They also seemed uninterested in pursuing money through federal programs designed to ameliorate concerns about government interference. The rescue mission in Phoenix seems more independent from government (at all levels) than those in New York or Nashville.

Nashville

Like Phoenix, Nashville has experienced a high number of migrants in search of work who, when work fails to materialize, are left isolated without familial contacts and social support (U.S. Conference of Mayors 2007). Not a great deal has been written about homelessness in Nashville, but a notable exception in the late 1980s (B. Lee 1989) also pinpointed other causes. Barrett Lee (1989) argues that the 1980s increase in the homeless population had become more visible as single-room-occupancy hotels were demolished in the process of urban redevelopment, and more vulnerable people were forced to sleep on the street. He also notes a change in the composition of the homeless population by the late 1980s, with more women, elderly people, and African Americans than previously. More recently, according to HUD (2008), the city experienced a 22.2 percent increase in its shelter population and an 18 percent decrease in its unsheltered population between 2006 and 2007 (table 5.9). This in part reflects the efforts of recent mayor Bill Purcell (1999–2007) and current mayor Karl Dean to address chronic homelessness in line with federal efforts (City of Nashville 2004; U.S. Conference of Mayors 2007). The Mayor's Commission to End Chronic Homelessness has focused its efforts on helping Nashville's providers improve medical access, family care, and shelter capacity, so it is possible that the divergent numbers (sheltered and unsheltered) simply reflect a transition of many people from the streets to emergency shelters. But the figures also reflect a gross undercount that should be viewed skeptically. According to the recent U.S. Conference of Mayors (2007) report, Nashville's actual level of homelessness (9,688 according to the report's estimate) is four times the federal estimate (2,156). The city's shelters routinely turn away homeless people for the night because they are operating at capacity. The city does not operate any shelters of its own but does try to facilitate placement and provide some funding for local nonprofits, including the Nashville Rescue Mission. The Nashville Rescue Mission contains over a third of the city's shelter beds and is arguably its most important provider of this sort.

Located just south of downtown on Lafayette Street, the Nashville Rescue Mission (NRM) is an impressively large organization. It has an annual budget of $6.8 million, with "not a dime of it from the government," noted an adamant staff member interviewed for this project (see table 5.10). Founded in 1954, the NRM provides a range of services including a chapel, career counseling, a food pantry, a soup kitchen, and an emergency shelter. Chapel is required for receipt of NRM services, but it has recently tried to be more accommodating of people of different faiths. One staff person, eager to counter the perception that NRM is not pluralistic, stated, "We just had a Buddhist and two Muslims in our program." Interviews with staff revealed no great conflicts with local government, but the aforementioned adamant stance toward refusing government funding spoke volumes, as did the firm belief that NRM's brand of service was superior to that provided by secular nonprofit and government operations. The NRM provides over 1,500 meals per day for the region's needy. It also provides 638 beds for the homeless, which constitute 36.1 percent of HUD's shelter estimate for the city.

In general, Nashville's rescue mission is more central to the safety net of its city than are the New York and Phoenix missions. Despite some evidence of NRM defiance toward government funding, the city relies on the organization as a provider for over a third of its homeless population. It is also interesting that during interviews NRM personnel expressed much less ambivalence regarding the role of faith in the provision of their services, as compared to mission personnel in New York and Phoenix. NRM personnel had a much clearer position about the boundaries between their care and that provided by the state.

RESCUE MISSIONS AS VEHICLES OF NEOLIBERALISM?

Gospel rescue missions provide a way to reduce government welfare expenditures and individualize poverty in a manner that aligns with neoliberal theory. So while most have been around for decades and the motivations of rescue mission staff may be complex, varied, and anything but monolithic, the form of care provided by such institutions fits very comfortably within the logic of religious neoliberalism and has been promoted actively by ideologues at the national level.

The survey conducted for this chapter reveals a number of findings that illuminate the role of FBOs, particularly rescue missions, in a context of neoliberalizing governance. First, the survey results underscore the fact that many of the mission personnel hold the perspective that poverty is a function of individual and spiritual failure. Unlike staff at the more moderate faith-related shelters and secular nonprofits, rescue mission staff do not generally see themselves as part of a larger social service picture that includes the secular governmental world. Not only did many respondents express the feeling that their brand of service was superior to that provided by government; many also felt that the latter actually contributed to the problem of poverty. Many rescue missions refuse on this basis to receive government funds that restrict their messages concerning individual and spiritual poverty. Explicit federal efforts to promote FBOs—Charitable Choice, the Faith-Based Initiative, and the Compassion Capital Fund—have been relatively ineffective, but in many ways this reflects how perfectly rescue missions fit into a neoliberal imaginary. As many neoliberals have pointed out, government-funded FBO social services do not differ greatly from government-provided social services. The ideologically pure neoliberal favors FBOs as independent replacements for, rather than government-funded supplements to, publicly provided services (see Ziegler 2005 and Sager 2006 for such ideologically pure statements).

But while rescue missions may stimulate the neoliberal imagination in purely ideational ways, it would be incorrect to assume that their practices and influence are felt evenly across the landscape of American homelessness. The cases studied illustrate the uneven geography of this saturation. The depth and nature of the welfare state as it existed under midcentury Keynesianism in each locality has deeply influenced the ways in which rescue missions are, or are not, being relied upon today. Though there are still serious gaps in coverage, New York's system of government-run, secular nonprofit, and sectarian nonprofit shelters is the most comprehensive, and rescue missions form only a small part of it. Even rescue mission officials in New York expressed ambivalence about the way forward, in contrast to those in Nashville and Phoenix, who were defiant in their criticism of government-provided support of almost any kind. In Phoenix, the current nonprofit shelter system is so incomplete that public officials admit that as much as one-third of the homeless population could not, even in theory, be accommodated. The PRM seems functionally separate from the local government, which relies more on secular nonprofits. The rescue mission in Nashville is the most thoroughly integrated into the "official" policy of care and houses more than a third of the shelter population. Shelter officials in Nashville seemed comparatively more adamant that their form of service is superior to government, and they seemed to have the best relationship with city hall of the three cases. The profiles illustrate, above all, that the safety net has become increasingly faith-saturated in a variety of locations, but that this is highly uneven, greatly dependent on the locally constructed nature of the welfare state.

Gospel rescue missions have a complicated political history in the United States, one that has been recently woven into the logic of religious neoliberalism. Their longstanding aversion to secular welfare and government aid coupled with their emphasis on personal responsibility, cloaked in scripture, make for a mutually beneficial ideational union with neoliberal policy. The fact that such policies have led to a growing reliance on rescue missions has instantiated this union in uneven but highly specific ways for homeless populations in U.S. cities. The spatiality of this union complicates any simple description, or dismissal, of faith-based agencies as vehicles of religious neoliberalism.

CHAPTER SIX

Religious Neoliberalism as Default

It has been more than five years since Hurricane Katrina demolished much of the physical and social infrastructure of New Orleans, but it remains for some a symbolic epicenter of religious neoliberalism, as the federal government famously turned to religious entities — places of worship and religious organizations — to deal with the human devastation wrought by the storm. The reliance on these entities was passive at first (the federal government was simply not doing what it had done in the past, so such groups picked up the slack), then systematic — once pressured into acting, the federal government positioned itself as a clearinghouse and voice for religious groups. The events surrounding Hurricane Katrina thus constitute a symbolically powerful instance of religious neoliberalism, one that helps reinforce the central ideas of this book.

On Monday, August 29, 2005, much of the world tuned in to watch one of the most surreal televised broadcasts of a "natural" disaster ever captured. As Hurricane Katrina bore down on the city of New Orleans, cameras captured initially very typical scenes of reporters in rain ponchos on abandoned piers trying to show viewers how windy and rainy hurricanes can be. But as the eye of the storm moved away and the clouds began to part, the scene turned to one of collective horror as broadcasts showed people atop buildings begging for their lives, and a government that seemed unable or unwilling to help.

Almost a month later, Michael Brown, then director of the Federal Emergency Management Agency (FEMA) and now disgraced icon of the debacle, was called before the U.S. Congress to testify on what had gone wrong (Brown 2005). If his initial response to the storm had seemed irresponsible and incompetent, the tenor of his response during the congressional testimony had taken on a certainty rooted more in ideology than in fecklessness. His comments seemed to affirm the growing chorus of critics who had framed the government nonresponse as a "violation of the social contract" or ideologically motivated social Darwinism. If the people of New Orleans were too ignorant to leave the city before the storm hit, then it was their fault that they were trapped. But there was something else in these statements that did not receive nearly as much attention by critics, then or since: his invocation of churches and religious organizations like the Salvation Army as the "proper" first responders in such disasters. This sentiment is intriguing, not least because if Brown was simply revealing a hidden ideological inclination for neoliberalism, his response about why the government behaved the way it did would likely echo this position, especially with the benefit of afterthought and the enormous political cover offered by neoliberal think tanks who were crafting such a position.

What does it say about the politics of neoliberalism if faith-based organizations (not charities more broadly) are postulated as idealized alternatives to a government safety net? Why, in other words, invoke the benefits of organizations that might not fit the largely secular plank of neoliberalism as articulated through its forefathers like Hayek and Friedman or their institutional offspring like the CATO Institute, the American Enterprise Institute (AEI), and the Heritage Foundation? The latter collectively issued hundreds of press releases after Hurricane Katrina arguing simply that responding to the aftermath was not the government's responsibility, with little or no mention of how churches and religious organizations might be of assistance. Why would Brown not simply invoke nonprofits in a more general sense, like CATO, AEI, and the Heritage Foundation did? Why single out religious institutions as the "proper" first responders? Was Brown demonstrating a more complicated politics than the classic narrative of neoliberalism? Or was he simply backtracking—trying to show that he had had a plan after all—when faced with the question of why his office so publicly and completely failed? Or was the type of "solution" (FBOs, as Brown suggested) a mere afterthought to the central goal of FEMA, namely, minimizing or eliminating the federal government's role in such tragedies? Given the large number of articles, books, essays, and reports written about the U.S. government's role in post-Katrina New Orleans, it is somewhat surprising that this particular angle has not been covered at length. This chapter attempts to discern the role of faith in the neoliberal reconstruction of post-Katrina New Orleans. The years since the event have yielded a large body of literature and a post-Katrina experience substantial enough to begin meaningfully addressing this question.

The central thesis of this chapter is that Katrina revealed a wrinkle in the ideal of neoliberal normativity, one that has been implied, but not fully elaborated, in the existing literature. The events and their aftermath revealed not only the ideal of charity-centered welfare and relief but also a moralizing dimension that conformed closely to that of a select number of faith-based organizations. The situation also revealed the practical and philosophical limits of merging the logic of religion-centered welfare with a highly devolved state. Understanding this wrinkle in the ideational landscape of neoliberalism is key to understanding both the processes that occurred on the ground in New Orleans in 2005 and the temporal and geographical dynamism of neoliberalism more generally.

FINDING NEOLIBERALISM IN THE KATRINA PLAN

Hurricane Katrina became an object lesson for researchers of neoliberalism in large part because the event laid bare a number of neoliberal assumptions, chief among them the idea that charities, not the state, should assume responsibility for human welfare. The first metaphorical wave of this research and critique arrived almost immediately after the literal first wave of Katrina's storm surge. In an impressively comprehensive essay, noted political economist Mike Davis (2005) released a scathing rebuke of the government nonresponse to the storm, and how, even after the fact, the rebuilding was being managed by think-tank ideologues at the AEI and the Heritage Foundation in Washington. One of the first orders of business was, as Davis points out, to relax the regulations requiring private companies to pay prevailing wages—regulations that had been targeted by these think tanks for decades. Other political economists like Jamie Peck (2006a, 2006b) wrote real-time accounts of the scramble by the federal government to mitigate the public relations disaster that Katrina had become, on the one hand, while mobilizing ideological forces to reassemble New Orleans according to a neoliberal plan, on the other. Still others, like center-left scholar-politician Michael Ignatieff criticized the federal government for leaving its citizens to their own devices, that is, by leaving individuals to fend for themselves. In his widely discussed essay in the *New York Times Magazine*, Ignatieff (2005) argued that the government's response constituted no less than a violation of the social contract. Together, this body of work constituted a scathing indictment of neoliberal governance—both the initial indifference to helping citizens under duress and the subsequent effort to roll out a set of policies that would rebuild New Orleans as a whiter, more market-friendly, less government-oriented place. Several themes in this literature are worth revisiting.

Foremost among these themes was the indictment of efforts by the Bush administration to exploit the storm's aftermath as an opportunity to deregulate and make New Orleans more business friendly. As Kevin Fox Gotham and Miriam Greenberg note, New Orleans became a laboratory for

> a variety of neoliberal redevelopment policies and tax subsidies directed to stimulating private investment. The use of enterprise zones and CDBGs reflects an entrenched ideology that the promotion of "free markets" is the most effective means of promoting urban recovery and rebuilding. This market-centered approach has been enforced "top-down" by a federal government averse to a strong public sector and direct outlay programs, and propagated by entrepreneurial city and state governments and public-private partnerships seeking to use post-disaster rebuilding as an opportunity to enhance their cities' competitiveness and business climate. (2008, 1055)

Government intervention was used, in other words, to roll out neoliberalism in the form of business-friendly tax, labor, and regulatory changes. Recent literature has also focused on how a paternalistic nonprofit system rather than direct government aid was unleashed on the notoriously "unruly" population of New Orleans (Katz 2008; Lipsitz 2006). Cindi Katz linked the diversion of resources and authority to nonprofits to a broader trend within neoliberalizing capitalism:

> The paternalism of the non-profit industrial complex is in some cases so severe that it recalls the colonial mindset that has plagued this part of the U.S. south for centuries. The stink of the sentiment that "these people cannot govern themselves" is no more palatable coming from NGOs than those previously in power, however well intentioned they might be. Under the last few decades of capitalist neoliberalism, moreover, these organizations and their state collaborators have increasingly professionalized their operations, defanging a lot of activism in the process. (2008, 25)

George Lipsitz (2006) goes even further, depicting the government response to the storm as akin to its actions in the Iraq war. Through the vehicle of nonprofits, who would demand "accountability" and not settle for providing mere "handouts," the federal government was able to impose a form of neoliberal punishment on those who dared to think that they were entitled to help from their government.

A third theme in the literature dealt with the ostensibly planned nature of the government's response. This ranged from accusations of benign neglect — by, for example, arguing that the gutting of FEMA a few years earlier left the government vulnerable to such a tragedy — to accusations of something more sinister: a "shock" program designed to discipline New Orleans (Klein 2007; Lipsitz 2006; Peck 2006a). Naomi Klein (2007) links the government response to a well-tested method on the right of exploiting "natural" disasters to "shock" systems that have become "too socialistic." Citing a long line of neoliberals who have made it their life's work to assemble ideas that would be used as alternatives in such moments of crisis, Klein documents how the efforts of various think tanks, who long viewed New Orleans as a symbol of Keynesian excess, trickled down (or up) to politicians voting on policy. It is no coincidence, she (and others) argue, that the first positive steps taken by the federal government involved the condemnation of public housing and the relaxation of labor standards. The storm created political cover to impose what had until that point been neoliberal fantasies conjured up in the hallways of the CATO, Manhattan, and American Enterprise Institutes. The variety of policy propositions offered by think-tank fellows in the days following the storm gives credence to the "shock theory." Many of the proposals had nothing to do with the storm itself but were tangential ideas that had been incubating in think tanks for years. Apparently the storm and its aftermath provided ample opportunity to present them as solutions. Among the many proposals offered were calls to impose a federal government disaster spending cap that could be overridden only by a supermajority in Congress (Boaz 2005), eliminate the strategic petroleum reserve (Taylor and Doren 2005), disallow Congress any authority over FEMA (Bandow 2005), deregulate the insurance industry so it could better cover residents (Balko 2005; Grace and Klein 2007), privatize the Army Corps of Engineers (Edwards 2005), and eliminate tariffs on Mexican cement and Canadian lumber (Harper 2006). The government may not have literally planned the storm, but by allowing it to serve as justification for downsizing the state and by deferring to neoliberal think tanks, government officials could engage in a planned deconstruction of New Orleans's Keynesian safety net, according to this line of thought.

In short, Hurricane Katrina became an enlightening case study for researchers of neoliberalism. A vast, interesting, critical literature has emerged to help understand the various dimensions of this event and its implications for geography, neoliberalism, and political movements more generally. But while there is a substantial literature on the geography of neoliberalism generally, and the neoliberalism laid bare by Hurricane Katrina more specifically, very little of it has focused on the role of religious charities or the idea of faith more generally in the political development of neoliberalism, in New Orleans or elsewhere.

FINDING FAITH IN THE KATRINA PLAN

The invocation and promulgation of neoliberalism is not the only theme that can be found in retrospectives on the Katrina government response. There was also a variety of invocations of the divine. In addition to the aforementioned continued references to churches and other faith-based entities as more appropriate first responders by FEMA director Brown, an almost macabre sentiment also emerged on the Right linking "God's will" to New Orleans's "sins." This took two forms.[1] First and most immediate were the public proclamations that God was punishing New Orleans for its vices. The most famous of these comments were made by religious conservatives Jerry Falwell and John Hagee, who attributed the storm to divine retribution for abortion and gay pride parades, respectively. But more-serious analysts also seemed comfortable invoking the notion that the sins of New Orleans played a part in either the storm itself or the government's response to it. Writing, for example, more than a month after the storm, Acton Institute fellow Eric Schansberg (2005) revealed his formulaic explanation for the events surrounding Katrina. "Natural disaster," he remarks, "plus government ineptitude plus sin equals a debacle of biblical proportions." He goes on to argue that only charities can solve the problems that sin helped to cause in New Orleans, because they are "more effective, more efficient, and can focus on the spiritual as well as the material concerns of the needy."

The second form of introducing the divine into discourses about the situation in New Orleans was the assertion that God triggered a rollback of Keynesian excess through the storm. After learning that the storm had finally destroyed much of the public housing in New Orleans that he and his colleagues had spent decades trying to demolish through policy, Republican congressman Richard Baker noted blithely: "We finally cleaned up public housing in New Orleans. We couldn't do it, but God did" (quoted in Lipsitz 2006). Such direct invocations of "God's will" were paralleled by subtler inferences that the storm was a blessing, in that it shook up an untenable situation. It deconcentrated the poor, or it "cleaned the slate" in New Orleans so that the government could finally let certain parts of the city go un-rebuilt. Largely, however, these comments, made by broad proponents of neoliberalism or narrow defenders of the Bush administration, remained fragmentary. None were part of formal statements linking the divine to the storm or of official reports explicitly identifying faith-oriented organizations as the best possible responders to the crisis.

These casual invocations of the divine aside, there was also a more deliberate effort to rely on charities, particularly religious charities, in the aftermath of the storm. Exploring this effort, and in particular those charities positioned most explicitly as alternatives to government, reveals the ways in which this picture differed from the classical neoliberal narrative. It is clear that faith-based organizations, particularly those relying minimally on governmental support, were favored as "first responders" (and subsequent responders) by the federal government. First, there was a demonstrated effort to bring FEMA in line with the trend toward faith-based delivery of services that marked the first term of the Bush administration. Without elaborating with too many details, the Bush administration's Faith-Based Initiative aimed to loosen federal restrictions on which religious groups could contract with the government to provide social services. One of the first related acts was an executive order requesting that all federal agencies review their contracting practices to explore "obstacles" to faith-based contracting. Shortly thereafter, faith-based offices were set up in five federal agencies to oversee efforts to funnel more money to faith-based agencies and curtail regulation that might hinder them. Though FEMA was not part of this initial wave of agencies, Joseph Allbaugh, its first director under Bush, boasted to Congress only a few months later about how receptive the agency had been to utilizing faith-based organizations for work that was once performed only by the government. Speaking in direct reference to federal efforts to assist with the Seattle earthquake of 2001, he explained FEMA's embrace of faith-oriented delivery:

> President Bush's compassionate conservatism is a hallmark of his core philosophy. The President is promoting faith-based organizations as a way to achieve compassionate conservatism. Not only does FEMA work with the faith-based organizations that I mentioned, but FEMA's Emergency Food and Shelter Program is the original Faith-Based Initiative and is a perfect fit with President Bush's new approach to helping the poor, homeless and disadvantaged. Through this program, FEMA works with organizations that are based in the communities where people need help the most. (Allbaugh 2001)

Allbaugh went on to elaborate on FEMA's receptiveness to this type of delivery and speculated that this would continue into the future. FEMA's reliance on nongovernmental entities, religious or not, only intensified after September 11, as the agency was demoted from its independent cabinet-level status, subsumed under the new Department of Homeland Security (DHS), and had its resources cut as DHS focused on other matters. FEMA moved from being a cooperative ally of the Faith-Based Initiative to becoming partially dependent on FBOs after this capacity-cutting restructuring.

Second, the federal government's commitment to FBOs was also highlighted in the fact that FBOs were a crucial part of the federal "solution" to the crisis. As the storm was making landfall on August 29, FEMA released a memo encouraging donations to NGOs as a response to the storm. "Volunteer organizations are seeking cash donations to assist victims of Hurricane Katrina in Gulf Coast states . . . [to] . . . provide a wide variety of services, such as clean up, child-care, housing repair, crisis counseling, sheltering and food," noted the memo (FEMA 2005). The document, later removed from FEMA's website after the media began to turn against the administration, then went on to list twenty-four organizations to which the public should donate money. Fully nineteen (79 percent) of the organizations listed were faith based, some of which, such as Pat Robertson's Operation Blessing, operated with openly sectarian forms of service delivery.[2]

The memo was released well before the cacophony of criticism about FEMA's woefully inadequate response. Far from somehow failing to activate, the agency had made its intent clear from the start. As the White House later clarified, the public was mistaken to assume that FEMA was in charge of the same types of activities as it had been under the Clinton administration. Bush's FEMA was in charge of unleashing "armies of compassion," not providing direct assistance to disaster victims (*Boston Globe* 2005). This sentiment was supported publicly by conservative politicians like Alabama senator Jeff Sessions, who responded to criticism about government inaction by arguing, "FEMA will never be large enough to deal with a hurricane of this size, and we wouldn't want them to" (quoted in *Boston Globe* 2005). Though the FEMA memo was eventually removed, likely because of public outcry and administration embarrassment, the federal inclination toward using the state as a clearinghouse for faith-based organizations continued through other vehicles, including but not limited to the Department of Housing and Urban Development (HUD). HUD continued to use its website years after the storm to redirect interested readers to donate to independent organizations — twenty-six of which were religiously affiliated, and most of which were being touted as providing services once provided by HUD. In general, it was clear that FEMA and other federal agencies had been restructured around the concept of relying more on the third sector, particularly religious NGOs, to provide services that government had provided until the recent past. Hurricane Katrina revealed this deliberate restructuring more than it revealed a lack of competence (though it revealed that too). The federal nonresponse to Katrina and the heavy reliance on religious organizations reflected an element of planning — at least to the extent that Bush administration officials expected FBOs to be the safety net in the first place.

It would take several years, however, to determine the extent of this reliance and how such responses differed, if at all, from those provided by secular NGOs or the government. The Government Accountability Office (GAO) produced several reports in 2006 that evaluated the Katrina experience and concluded that the federal government must improve monitoring, performance measures, and accountability for government partnerships with FBOs, as it was difficult to discern where much of the Katrina money went (GAO 2006; Fagnoni 2005). In 2008, the U.S. Department of Health and Human Services commissioned a study by the Urban Institute (UI) to extensively examine the role of nonprofits — religious and secular — during and after the Katrina disaster (De Vita et al. 2008). It remains the most comprehensive and systematic study conducted on the topic. The research was based on a sample of 202 nonprofits involved in Katrina disaster response, 120 (59.4 percent) of which self-identified as religious, most of these congregation based. The research also relied on eight in-depth case studies.

The findings provide a comprehensive portrait of the faith-related neoliberal model used to respond to Katrina. Organizations describe having provided a range of services once delivered by federal agencies like FEMA. These services ranged from fulfilling immediate needs — food, water, emergency shelter — to longer-term counseling, rebuilding, and community building. Secular nonprofits were more likely than their religious counterparts to be involved in longer-term activities. A number of other findings also seem particularly salient here. First, all faith-based organizations relied heavily on volunteer labor, and two-thirds of the FBOs had no experience with disaster relief before the storm. Second, faith-based organizations were significantly less likely to rely on government funds than secular NGOs and much more likely to receive individual donations. Third, relatively few FBOs worked with state or local government; secular NGOs were more likely to do so (23 percent versus 10 percent). Fourth, FBOs were more likely to ally with other faith-based organizations than with secular or governmental entities. In general, the federal government's response centrally involved nongovernmental entities and particularly favored faith-based organizations. The resulting service net was poorly coordinated, full of redundancies, and a poor replacement for services theretofore provided by federal agencies like FEMA. The most common challenges cited by NGOs, secular and sectarian alike, were insufficient supplies, poor service coordination, and poor communication. Problems notwithstanding, the overall response aligned perfectly with the neoliberal notion that governments should not meddle in social assistance.

FAITH-BASED ORGANIZATIONS AS ALTERNATIVES TO THE STATE

Like most studies of faith-based organizations, the UI report on the Katrina response focused on organizations that were at least amenable to the idea of accepting government funding, even if they did not actually receive it. But if we accept that the core idea of neoliberalism is not that government should contract out all its social assistance functions, but rather that it should completely devolve responsibility to the nonprofit sector (with little or no government funding), then such organizations as those studied by the UI do not give a clear indication of the role that nonprofits, religious or otherwise, played in the neoliberalization of New Orleans. At best they provide a picture of a shadow state growing through a series of nonprofit intermediaries in a time of crisis. In order to explore the role within neoliberalism, we must turn to organizations that have built their identity around the idea of being an alternative to, rather than a recipient of, government funding.

This is no easy task. While much of the political rhetoric during the Bush years was aimed at positioning FBOs as a more compassionate and efficient alternative that should replace state-centered welfare, most faith-based organizations, as discussed earlier, do not deliberately align themselves with such politics. In addition to those receiving government money (and thus serving as an extension of the interventionist state), many have actually functioned historically as service vehicles in the absence of state welfare (not as an alternative to it). This is particularly the case in New Orleans, where, for example, churches in the large African American community have provided social services for their congregations for decades, because the state would not do so. Many others have had close relationships with government funding — serving as culturally legitimate deliverers of government welfare — during the twentieth century and have routinely formed the institutional platform for agitating for more, not less, welfarist redistribution. So despite the fantasies of think-tank ideologues and some in the Bush administration, the New Orleans faith-based community was not eagerly awaiting the opportunity to finally take over where the government had failed. Most FBOs either had an existing relationship with the state, operated out of necessity where the government would or could not and displayed no antagonism toward state-based welfare, or were actively agitating for the state to expand its role. Conceptually, organizations providing assistance in the absence of government intervention must be distinguished from those that deliberately position themselves as independent alternatives to government-based welfare (or broader interventions). The former operate independently due to necessity, whereas the latter have a critique of the welfare state at their core. Unfortunately (for analytical purposes), there are few ideal-type institutions completely immune from government funding and the regulations regarding the scope and type of care that are usually attached. There are, however, organizations that have built their identity around their independence from government and are able to attract donations on the basis of this putative independence. The New Orleans branches of two such projects are revealing examples: the New Orleans Area Habitat for Humanity (NOAHH) and the New Orleans Rescue Mission (NORM).

These organizations are very different on the surface — one designed to provide homeownership possibilities to the working poor, the other to provide emergency shelter and services to the abjectly poor (Hackworth 2009b, 2010b). But despite their obvious differences, they also share important similarities that justify their inclusion in a study of this sort. First, they both avoid government resources and in many cases position themselves rhetorically as the antithesis of government social assistance. This stance continues in their rhetoric but has softened in practice, particularly in extreme circumstances like the Katrina events. Second, they possess very limited capacity, in part because of their reluctance to accept a more consistent stream of funding from government. The trait of limited capacity is not unusual in the NGO world, but it is notable in this case given how routinely NOAHH and NORM are framed as plausible solutions to New Orleans's housing problems by the media and political figures despite these limitations. Third, they both emphasize, more than most FBOs that partner directly with government, an individually oriented, quasi-Calvinist approach.[3] This approach emphasizes personal responsibility, rather than social solutions, and insists that hard work is the singular key to solving their clients' problems. And fourth, they both embody forms of care that originated elsewhere and were imported to New Orleans. Neither NORM nor NOAHH is firmly ensconced in the rich network of African American churches that have helped the city's poor (often with assistance from government) for decades. NORM and NOAHH are idealized models whose putative "other" is not just government-based welfare but also the hundreds of secular and religious organizations contracting with government to deliver welfare in New Orleans. Research on NORM and NOAHH for this chapter consisted of interviews with staff and an exploration of secondary materials and archives, all of which were mined to focus on (1) their funding model; (2) their responsibilities since Katrina; (3) how their model differs from that of other FBOs and the government; and (4) their relationship with government.

The New Orleans Rescue Mission

The New Orleans Rescue Mission, founded in 1989, is located near the Louisiana Superdome in downtown New Orleans. According to the State of Louisiana (2009), it is the second largest emergency shelter facility in the city. Since its establishment, it has offered a range of services from shelter and meals for men, women, and families, to medical care, job training, and a transitional work program. Though most of the other eighteen emergency shelter facilities in the city have a religious orientation, NORM is distinct in both its strictness and its fundamentalist orientation. Like many rescue missions in the country, NORM has a policy of strict chapel attendance in exchange for these services. As a management-level respondent to an interview undertaken for this study stated bluntly, "If you want to eat, there is chapel service. That is biblical."

The size and range of NORM's services were curtailed dramatically following the storm, the most direct impact of which was the almost complete destruction of its main facility. As a result, 90 percent of its staff had to be laid off, and its capacity to house and provide services was severely undermined. Prior to Hurricane Katrina, NORM housed approximately 250 men and 20 women per night in its facility. For many months after the storm, NORM had no capacity, but with the help of mortgage giant Ameriquest, the government of Qatar, and an army of church volunteers from across the country, it is now able to house 140 men and 20 women per night. The men sleep in a large, temperature-controlled tent (NORM 2009). The donor base was similarly decimated by the storm, shrinking from a pre-Katrina high of 28,000 to 3,500 after the storm. The organization's erstwhile reluctance to draw on government funding has softened somewhat in recent years as the city, state, and federal governments, desperate to deal with a rapidly growing homeless population in a city trying to rebuild its tourism sector, struggle for solutions. According to interviews conducted with NORM staff, the rescue mission has helped "solve" the problem of the homeless causing trouble in the French Quarter, the city's main tourism draw: "They [the city] were having problems with homeless living near the French Quarter and raising a ruckus and we helped them out with that." Also according to staff familiar with the situation, this accomplishment led to "stronger support" from federal officials like Senator Mary Landrieu and larger organizations like the New Orleans Chamber of Commerce. Partially as a result of these developments, the city recently granted NORM a no-strings-attached infusion of $165,000 (approximately 20 percent of NORM's annual budget) to assist with its operating expenses. In the past, such financial help would often come with stipulations about how it could be spent, so organizations like NORM, keen on maintaining their religious bent, rarely requested such resources. They are now nearing pre-Katrina capacity levels, and their donor base is slowly returning. But NORM's story, and especially the city's reliance on it to "solve" its homeless problem, raise a series of critical issues.

It is important to recognize that the rescue mission model—reliant as it is on individual and corporate donations—is highly vulnerable to fluctuations in revenue and volunteer interest. It is also difficult to build capacity in such situations. Even at its height, NORM housed only 270 people per night. According to the estimates of its own management (revealed through interviews), which are somewhat lower than others, there were at least 6,000 homeless people in New Orleans before the storm. After the chaos inflicted by Katrina, they posit that the city's homeless population is now at least 12,000 (see also HUD 2008, 12). It is, of course, neither NORM's responsibility nor its stated aim to house all of these people, but most other nonprofits and government-run shelters experienced a similar decimation following the storm, so its experience is perhaps reflective of a wider trend. Moreover, the city, with its own capacity stripped and desperate to revive the once-thriving tourism economy, is looking for inexpensive solutions. NORM has emerged as one of those "solutions," to the extent that it provides a place that draws homeless people away from the French Quarter.

But the use of NORM as a "solution" to the city's homeless problem is more than just a question of providing shelter for the lowest possible cost. It also raises a basic philosophical problem about ostensibly secular governments (at various levels) relying on such openly sectarian organizations to provide emergency shelter. NORM, like all rescue missions, is motivated by a fundamentalist reading of the Bible. The rescue mission emphasizes the individual causes of poverty and provides individualized "solutions" to those problems. Those who devote their time, money, and energy to gospel rescue missions (GRMS) see their role as healing troubled individuals who have lost faith in God or strayed from core personal principles. It is, of course, their right to advocate such an approach, but the long-standing tension that characterizes government funding of sectarian organizations becomes intensified in certain contexts, specifically those in which crises like Katrina are combined with extant trends like neoliberalism that hollow out government, giving officials little choice but to turn to anyone who will provide.

New Orleans Area Habitat for Humanity

The New Orleans Area Habitat for Humanity was founded in 1983 and has built over 200 homes for working poor residents of the city and surrounding area (NOAHH 2009). Much of its building activity has taken place in the Upper Ninth Ward, in Jefferson Parish on the west bank, and the Hollygrove neighborhoods, and these areas continue to receive attention due to the concentration of flood damage there. When Katrina hit in 2005, the organization emerged as a high-profile "solution" for a public that had grown weary of government indifference to the housing problem in the city. NOAHH's volunteering capacity and donations swelled dramatically after the storm, with many university students, interested citizens, and politicians still making the trek to New Orleans to volunteer. Politicians of different ideological backgrounds, from Bobby Jindal (the current governor of Louisiana) to President Barack Obama, have already volunteered to help build on a construction site. As of 2008, NOAHH had completed 100 post-Katrina houses and was building another 160 — remarkable numbers given that its output in twenty-two years of work prior to the storm was around 200 homes (NOAHH 2009). In 2006, it was the largest building permit applicant (nonprofit or for-profit) in New Orleans, and it has enjoyed the assistance of over sixty thousand volunteers since the storm.

The extensive damage caused by the storm has also spawned a number of high-profile efforts to generate publicity for the organization. Longtime Habitat icons former president Jimmy Carter and wife, Rosalynn, for example, sponsored a "work project week" during which NOAHH built seven houses and started another twenty-five in one week in May 2008. According to its communications director, Aleis Tusa, NOAHH is also embarking on an attempt to build housing for displaced musicians, dubbed "Musicians' Village." The development, which is located in the Upper Ninth Ward, features a planned seventy-two-unit neighborhood, with one-third to one-half of the units intended for area musicians. In short, NOAHH has emerged as one of the most high-profile FBO housing providers in post-Katrina New Orleans. It has enjoyed extremely positive press and is routinely deployed in rhetoric as a positive antidote to "government failure" in the city. But a closer look at NOAHH's activities also reveals the stubborn capacity constraints and enduring philosophical concerns of having a religious organization so centrally responsible for rebuilding the broken city.

First and foremost, the organization is, by design, only able to help those who can become successful homeowners after the initial construction takes place. NOAHH is very open about income thresholds, which are between 35 and 60 percent of area median income — far above public housing thresholds (NOAHH 2009). Its criteria also note that applicants must be able to demonstrate need but also prove that they have secure employment and are able to repay Habitat's subsidized loan and any relevant taxes. They also must be willing to devote 350 hours of labor, submit to criminal background checks, and attend a series of seminars on credit and home maintenance. To this extent, NOAHH caters to a fairly narrow segment of the market — those who can afford a house payment but who do not qualify for any other government-subsidized program like FHA loans, who have 350 hours to devote to the construction of their house, and who are able to wait at least two years for the construction to be completed. Many of the homes destroyed in Katrina were owned by under- or unemployed people who had acquired their residence via inheritance. Formally qualifying for a loan, with or without the help of volunteers and sweat equity, is not a realistic solution for many in New Orleans.

This is perhaps nowhere more evident than in NOAHH's much-lauded Musicians' Village project. The intent with the village was to reserve up to one-third of the housing for resident musicians, but NOAHH's qualification model has proved difficult to adapt to the erratic income of even the most successful musicians. Many musicians have credit problems and highly variable incomes and thus are unable to qualify under Habitat's criteria. As of this writing, only one-quarter of the first phase of the village is actually going to be occupied by musicians, because Habitat has found it so difficult to fit them into its model (*New Orleans Times-Picayune* 2007a, 2007b). In response to the credit problems, free legal services were offered to those who did not qualify for a loan, with the goal of assisting them in eliminating old debts and removing negative items from credit reports. An additional step was to allow the musicians to use a schedule of upcoming performances as proof of income rather than their federal income tax returns. Musicians and other community activists have begun to complain not only that few of the intended recipients are actually receiving housing, but also that Habitat is benefiting from the *image* of housing such individuals even though the reality has not lived up to expectations.

A second tension revealed by Habitat's role in post-Katrina reconstruction deals with the role of government funding and the constitutional limitations attached to it. As mentioned earlier, Habitat for Humanity has long built its image on the idea of being an alternative to government-funded housing. For many years, it rejected any offering of government help and only recently began to accept in-kind support such as land donations or tax reductions. It recently applied for, and was awarded, an operating grant from HUD and increasingly accepts various forms of help from the state and the city (Aleis Tusa, interview with author, 2009). The recent warming to support from government is not isolated to New Orleans. The organization has tried in recent years to morph itself into a more mainstream nonprofit, open to a variety of funding sources including government (Hackworth 2009b; *New York Times* 2005).

It is difficult to interpret these recent changes and to know whether they will expand or contract in the future, but at the very least the closer relationship with government raises a series of familiar philosophical questions that are intrinsic when governments and religious organizations combine forces. What, for example, happens when the shadow state imposes a very particular set of behavior requirements on the social assistance that it provides? Though Habitat officials are open about their Christian roots, they are very careful to maintain a pluralistic stance about who can volunteer, donate, or receive their housing. But by the same token, they are not a value-free vehicle for housing delivery—they invoke a strongly individualist notion of "self-help." This is, of course, their right as an independent organization, but when the federal or any other level of government begins to fund such organizations, it becomes a tacit endorsement of their approach. When high-profile politicians choose to donate their time to a Habitat project, this tacit endorsement becomes a full-throated celebration of the approach. As Habitat's directors so routinely like to point out, they are not a "handout" (as in government welfare); they are a "hand up." It remains to be seen whether NOAHH's close relationship with government at various levels is a temporary arrangement born of the crisis inflicted by Katrina. But at the very least, the organization's carefully scripted brand and its high-profile participation in the "solution" to Katrina imply a form of third-sector workfare.

RELIGIOUS NEOLIBERALISM IN POLICY

The U.S. government reaction to Hurricane Katrina became an object lesson for a variety of scholars and public intellectuals, which is probably why so much has been written about the topic. Faith-based organizations—churches, nonprofits, and miscellaneous groupings of individuals—were a crucial part of the initial response, but comparatively little academic research has been devoted to studying their role specifically. FBOs helped in the immediate aftermath with housing, food, and water, and in the medium- and longer-term with transitional housing, counseling, and cleanup. Though many of these organizations were acting on their own mandates, it is also evident that the overall idea of involving FBOs so intimately with responsibilities once held by the federal government was planned.

FEMA showed an inclination to adhere to Bush's Faith-Based Initiative well before Katrina had developed in the mid-Atlantic. When it was restructured in 2003, FEMA's capacity as a vehicle of Keynesian disaster relief was stripped. The normative idea that churches ought to be first responders was merged with the reality that FEMA was no longer in a position to offer an alternative. When Katrina finally did strike, the federal nonresponse and incompetence became famous. FEMA, and the federal government more generally, framed themselves as helpless, encouraging citizens to donate money to (mostly religious) charities if they wanted to help. Even after a month of bad press and backtracking following the spread of this idea, FEMA director Michael Brown was still promoting the idea that churches, not the federal government, were responsible for helping people in need. The role of FBOs as venerated alternatives to the state was also promoted through less formal channels: via think-tank press releases, interviews, and press accounts documenting a level of care that seemed to counter the indifference of the government response. Antiwelfarist organizations enjoyed sanctification in the political and media atmosphere following Katrina, despite their dramatically undermined capacity in the wake of the storm. Though most religious nonprofits have at least a partial relationship with government funding and thus are on shaky ground should they seek to make broad ideological swipes at the government, the spirit of the independent FBO was embodied quite purely by Habitat for Humanity and the New Orleans Rescue Mission. Both enjoyed almost unequivocally positive press as compassionate first responders and were (and continue to be) routinely framed as alternatives to the government, even though both have very limited capacity and promote a very particular view of poverty and its solutions.

But what are we to make of this? Was this a case of "armies of compassion" (a favorite phrase of President Bush's) rallying to help those in need, or was it a vehicle to cloak the cornerstones of neoliberal governance—personal responsibility, a noninterventionist state, workfare—with the more widely palatable veneer of religion? Or is this a false dualism? Could it be that New Orleans revealed that faith is both a metaphysical motivator for individuals concerned about those in need, and a vehicle deliberately deployed by neoliberal think tanks, politicians, and some religious figures to institute a more resolutely neoliberal political economy? More research would be necessary to answer these questions with definitive clarity, but this analysis suggests a few themes worth considering. First, while FBOs are varied in their outlook, focus, and approach, they have been deployed as both ideas and actualized vehicles to promote particular projects like neoliberalism. This means that not all (or even the majority of) FBOs are passive facilitators of neoliberalism but rather that scholars should be careful to consider all the ways in which FBOs function. The notion that some FBOs function as anti-neoliberal political catalysts is well founded. The fact that they can be deployed for the exact opposite purpose deserves more scholarly attention. Second, the inclusion of FBOs in the neoliberal narrative raises a series of question that challenge the practical and philosophical limits of both religious welfare and the role of government. These questions present themselves most starkly in cases where the FBO is a putative replacement for the state and includes a moralizing dimension in its service. The broader literatures on neoliberalism and faith-based organizations—both very large but almost completely compartmentalized from each other—would benefit from a more serious consideration of these questions.

CHAPTER SEVEN

End Times for Religious Neoliberalism?

If this book had been written seven or eight years ago, it would have been tempting to conclude with some kind of statement about the inexorable march of religious neoliberalism in the United States — on how it would strengthen in the coming years and eventually dominate thinking on both religion and economy. The White House was occupied at the time by a self-professed conservative evangelical who seemed to embody the ideals of religious neoliberalism as well as anyone in recent memory. The Faith-Based Initiative was still active — experiencing some growing pains, but active — and working to build the capacity of small religious organizations to begin assuming more control over welfare. Faith in small government seemed omnipresent.

But if we fast-forward to the present, it would be disingenuous or delusional to suggest such uncontested hegemony today, and on reflection, it seems that it may also have been an overstatement to suggest that this was the case under Bush. Signs are everywhere today not only of the diminished credibility of neoliberalism as a worldview but also of the unraveling of the curious fusion of neoliberalism and religious conservatism that has dominated the Right throughout the past thirty years. Governments are being called upon to bail out sectors of the economy in a way that looks positively Keynesian. Many of the key figures of the Religious Right have died, been discredited, or gone bankrupt. So what are we to make of this? Has religious neoliberalism died?

The thesis of this chapter, and the overall conclusion of this book, is that religious neoliberalism is, and always has been, partial. It was not invented when George W. Bush was elected president and did not dissolve when he exited office eight years later. Neoliberalism represents a rationality that served to fuse hitherto disparate elements of the American Right and as such helped fuel electoral success for the better part of thirty years. But it contained the seeds of its own destruction — it proved ideationally divisive, not fusionist. It also appears to have been more limited than many scholarly considerations have thus far characterized it. It has never been the only rationality operating on the American Right, and one could in retrospect make the argument that it was not even the Right's core rationality. Rather, like all other rationalities, it is partial, and we can learn a great deal, not only about religious neoliberalism but about all metaconcepts within the political realm, by recasting it as such. Recognizing this, however, does not automatically or sensibly lead to the conclusion that it is irrelevant. It has been a powerful part, even if only part, of conservative identity formation since its genesis as a coherent idea four decades ago. We should neither overstate its importance nor prematurely pen its obituary.

WHITHER RELIGIOUS NEOLIBERALISM?

Though the rise of religious neoliberalism has had a palpable impact on social policy in the United States, even the most casual student of American public affairs today could persuasively argue that it would be misleading to end the story here. At least since 2006, it has been not the supporters of faith-based welfare who have stood out but rather the resurgence of its longtime detractors and even the emergence of internal defectors. The fissures exposed by a careful examination of religious neoliberalism are emblematic of larger fissures in the American Right that shed some light on the partiality of neoliberalism. The criticisms of the faith-based movement have been (and continue to be) as varied as the people making them.

Given the virtual lockstep loyalty of the evangelical Right to the Republican Party, perhaps the most surprising source of dissent first came from former Bush administration officials. David Kuo (2006), a former high-level official in the Office of Faith-Based and Community Initiatives (OFBCI), took the Bush administration to task for exploiting the loyalty of evangelicals. In particular, he argued that the administration misled the religious community about how much new money would go into the program and that many in the administration simply saw it as a vehicle for garnering African American votes (by favoring African American churches in the allocation of money). Kuo summarized his critique by suggesting that the administration viewed the evangelical community simply as "useful idiots" to be placated in superficial ways in exchange for electoral loyalty. But perhaps the most biting critique came from OFBCI's first director, John Dilulio, who revealed his early antipathy for the machinations of the Bush White House in an interview with *Esquire* magazine published shortly after his resignation (Suskind 2003). He conveyed exasperation with the administration's lack of interest in governing the faith-based program (or any other social program for that matter) in any serious fashion. He argued that the Bush White House was governed by ideology and its political advisor Karl Rove. DiIulio went on to profess his continued loyalty to the principles of faith-based social welfare and even Bush himself but dismay at the way that ideologues like Rove were able to set and execute the administration's agenda. Lew Daly (2006), a theological scholar who is otherwise supportive of the idea of faith-based welfare, lambasted the former administration's implementation, saying that it was a betrayal of the European principles (subsidiarity and sphere sovereignty) upon which it was ostensibly built.

And the political troubles did not end there. The chorus of criticism from ideological sympathizers was paralleled by criticism from more-predictable sources — the "liberal" media, critical scholars, and activists — whose ideas have recently gained increased political traction. The *New York Times* ran a series of scathing articles detailing the use and abuse of Faith-Based Initiative policies in the past several years (*New York Times* 2007a). They found instances of federal funds being used in explicitly religious ways, employees being dismissed for not holding the right religious or political views, and local zoning rulings being overridden — all traceable to changes made since the implementation of the Faith-Based Initiative began in 2001. Activist groups like Americans United for Separation of Church and State (AUSCS) also gained political traction toward the end of the Bush administration (AUSCS n.d.; Luchenitser 2002). The tenor of AUSCS's message was not surprising coming from a group with such a clear mandate, but it was perhaps more surprising that its outlook was beginning to resonate more broadly.

In the realm of predictable if previously ignored criticism has been the response of noted academics who were critical of the Faith-Based Initiative and its implementation (see among many others Chaves 2001a, 2001b, 2001c). It was not surprising that some academics were critical of the Faith-Based Initiative, but it is notable that the ideas this group had been voicing for years were now becoming part of a broader public discussion. And it would, of course, be an easily refuted exaggeration to suggest that the political ethos embodied by the Faith-Based Initiative, by the government's response to Hurricane Katrina, or by the broad antipathy for secular government assistance in the welfare arena were still hegemonic. One could seriously argue that the financial meltdown, the election of President Obama, and a more interventionist posture in Washington have rendered such assertions empty. Indeed, this is exactly the point of inspiration for the Tea Party movement — that government is becoming "socialist" and needs to be recaptured. Religious neoliberalism, particularly the idea of turning much of the welfare state over to FBOs, has been hobbled, to say the very least, by the events of the past several years.

To make matters worse for religious neoliberalism, the Religious Right experienced a parallel implosion that served to make it politically toxic in some corners. Most superficially important were the high-profile falls of several of the movement's most important ideological and political supporters. Those downfalls included but were not limited to Ted Haggard, former leader of the influential National Association of Evangelicals and prominent homophobe, for (eventually) admitting to having an affair with a male prostitute; Ralph Reed, founder of the Christian Coalition, for having a role in the Jack Abramoff lobbying scandal; and Tom Delay, an important fundraiser and supporter of the Religious Right, for being indicted for money laundering. These public downfalls were paralleled by fateful private battles within the evangelical community. One important rupture that emerged within the broad evangelical ranks is based on divisions over whether to broaden the base of issues upon which the community rests politically. Traditionalists continue to feel that the focus should remain on traditional wedge issues like gay marriage and abortion, while moderates are interested in broadening the focus to encompass issues of poverty, environmental change, immigration, and international affairs. The battle over whether to recognize global warming as a significant issue has been particularly divisive, pitting ancien régime evangelicals like James Dobson and Charles Colson against more moderate figures like Rick Warren, Richard Cizik (former vice president for governmental affairs at the NAE), and Duane Litfin (former president of Wheaton College) (Hagerty 2006).[1] These high-profile rifts and the downfall of many of the movement's most prominent advocates are a sharp departure from the relatively smooth rise to prominence that the movement experienced in the late 1990s and early years of the twenty-first century. Some of these matters are superficial, while some involve actual policy, but they have each contributed to splintering the once-unified political constituency on which the Faith-Based Initiative is built.

Downfalls, internal divisions, and mainstream scrutiny of its component camps are not the extent of the problems facing religious neoliberalism. Some on the Right have begun to question the logic of the union itself, in a mini-revival of the fusionist debates that challenged the Right in the 1950s and 1960s. One need only return to the midcentury work of Hayek to understand that the alliance of these two factions is neither perfectly logical (in a political sense) nor very old historically (Hayek 1960). Hayek, the forefather of modern neoliberalism, went to great lengths to distance himself from what he saw as the backward thinking of social conservatives, going so far as to devote a chapter of his opus to explaining, "Why I am not a conservative." As Ryan Sager more recently (2006) explains, the rift was fundamental, but strangely the Republican Party was able to avoid division for the better part of forty years. To be sure, as Sager points out, the arrangement between neoliberals and social conservatives "has always been more *Married with Children* than *Ozzie and Harriet*" (2006, 9), but the success of the Republican Party, and the Right in general, is in no small measure due to the durability of this unlikely union. This, Sager and others argue, could end very shortly if the Republican Party continues to stray from the values of small-government conservatism (i.e., neoliberalism). Sager, a former fellow at the CATO Institute, felt — before it was popular to do so — that the Bush administration brazenly turned a blind eye to how the expansion of government, the intrusion on civil liberties, and the complete disregard for the separation of church and state have alienated purist neoliberals. In effect, paralleling Kuo's argument, Sager was saying that economic conservatives — neoliberals — were being played as "useful idiots."

High-profile events like the intervention by Congress and the Bush administration to "save" the life of Terry Schiavo and the passage of the Patriot Act (praised by social conservatives but reviled by neoliberals as an intrusion upon civil liberties) exacerbated intra-Right tensions. These events bolstered the impression that the Bush administration was beholden to the social conservative Right and placed a wedge between the two broad factions of the Republican Party. But while these events were divisive of Republicans, it was the Faith-Based Initiative that caused the most public acrimony between the two sides. As Sager argues, "No one example, perhaps, could better illustrate the skills of Bush, Rove, and company as manipulators of the moral minority than the policy disappointment/political coup that has been the president's Faith-Based Initiative" (2006, 150). He contends that the initiative only superficially placated the evangelical Right while completely abandoning the neoliberal Right.[2] In addition to flirting with the imposition of a theocratic order that might jeopardize civil rights, he asserts, it used government funding to achieve its ends. As Jennifer Ziegler (2005) of the CATO Institute notes of the Faith-Based Initiative in 2005 during testimony to Congress:

> Just because something is a good idea does not mean it should be a government program. In the case of faith-based organizations, government involvement can easily kill the very entity it is trying to nurture. During the past decade, the federal government has recognized the successful results that come from social services delivered by civil society, including religious organizations. . . .
>
> Faith-based organizations are crucial members of civil society that need to replace the federal welfare system, not be dependent on it.

This sentiment certainly resonated among the neoliberal Right and threatened to undermine support for the Faith-Based Initiative in particular and religious neoliberalism more generally.

Whether this row is significant enough to rip apart the fabric of the Republican Party (as Sager suggests) is perhaps a question for a different book. But of primary interest here is the way in which it has revealed the differences in neoliberal and social conservative positions on social welfare. Neoliberals are eager to hand social services over to churches as a way of reducing the size of government, while social conservatives are interested in using government to reform the poor and the larger culture from which they feel poverty is spawned. Post-Bush Republican battles over the relative importance of social and spending issues have only made this division more public. Religious neoliberalism is obviously now more challenged, from within and without, than it has been for decades. But what are the implications of this development? Do the recent challenges mean the inevitable death of religious neoliberalism, or is this a temporary setback? Moreover, do the long-standing challenges that have been exposed mean that religious neoliberalism was never as strong or harmonious as it was once framed to be? Was it a political juggernaut or a paper tiger? Do recent polls that show a high degree of overlap between the Tea Party and the Religious Right (and the current Republican efforts to pander to both) mean that it is only a matter of time before a proud, public, and effective religious neoliberalism reemerges? Some insights can be gleaned by returning to the literature on secular neoliberalism, as it contains many parallels that help illuminate the trajectory of religious neoliberalism.

(SECULAR) NEOLIBERALISM AS PARTIAL

When highly deregulated credit markets nearly ground to a halt in 2008, pundits across the political spectrum began to invoke the specter of a possible depression. Most countries in the developed world reacted quickly. Stimulus funds were injected to generate a demand-sided bulwark against the turmoil. Regulatory measures were taken to stop the practices that had led to the fiasco. Banks with toxic assets were either nationalized or significantly bailed out. Even some of the true believers in the Bush administration embarked on a pathway that looked positively Keynesian, some even said "socialist"—banks were effectively bought by the federal government, capital was "injected," and few serious economists were talking about tax cuts or a balanced budget as a way out, initially at least. Neoliberal fantasies about balanced budgets and tax breaks for the wealthy finally seemed like irresponsible policies in this climate.

The first order of business for the Obama administration was to pass a stimulus bill, built largely on Keynesian principles. Funds to banks continue to flow, and regulatory measures were on the table for the first time in forty years. Some declared this series of events the death of neoliberalism. Others were more cautious but acknowledged the ideological blow that had been delivered. How can we understand this series of events and the academic and public reaction to them? Did neoliberalism die? Did the saints of neoliberalism — Reagan, Thatcher, Hayek — no longer have the answer to societal or economic problems? Do the recent successes of the Tea Party mean that this period was just temporary?

I do not want to diminish the importance of figures like Hayek, Reagan, and Thatcher or organizations like the CATO Institute, the Heritage Foundation, and AEI, but I do want to suggest that we remember that the ideas of neoliberalism are rooted in a much longer history than these figures or organizations, and that their influence was always partial even in their most powerful episodes. Declaring the death of neoliberalism in 2008 (or its rebirth in the form of the Tea Party) perpetuates the myth that it was absent before these figures and omnipresent during their high-water mark. Why is this important? Because neoliberalism did not originate with the neoliberal turn in the 1970s and onward. Its ideational foundations stretch back much further, to at least the classical liberals of the late eighteenth and early nineteenth centuries, and by some accounts back to the Reformation and even Greek civilization (Girvetz 1963; Hayek 1960). And though the ideas were less influential during Keynesian or socialist periods in many countries, they were not entirely extinct, just like the influences of Keynesianism and socialism have waxed and waned but never disappeared entirely. For example, a U.S. public housing policy from the 1950s could reasonably be called a "Keynesian" policy in the sense that it helped stimulate demand and create a welfarist safety net. But how are we to understand provisions that encouraged work and individuated poverty (Hackworth 2003) — many of which were justified by the same logic that purist neoliberals at the CATO Institute now employ? Similarly, what are we to make of modern-day workfare programs — clearly neoliberal in many senses — that are also justified or function as demand-side stimulators?

North American cities are ensconced in societies that have always been liberal in some sense — in some ways, they were founded on such principles. Neoliberalism, as I understand it, was initially an attempt by Hayek and Friedman, then by others, to effectively skip past the "egalitarian liberal" period and return with a vengeance to the unapologetic classical liberalism that accepted the brutality of markets as a virtue. So when cities adopted policies influenced by neoliberalism, they were not inventing the idea out of thin air. They were drawing on the legitimacy of established economists and think tanks that had built a narrative extracted directly from the classical liberalism upon which the United States and Canada were founded. The neoliberal turn was thus one of emphasis, not a qualitatively new idea. The so-called death of neoliberalism likewise must surely be interpreted as a shift in emphasis. Perhaps the virulent mean-spiritedness of the CATO Institute or Grover Norquist will become less popular, but it would be absurd to suggest that other ideas of neoliberalism will evaporate completely. The resurgence of religious neoliberalism cloaked as the Tea Party — with a public emphasis on antiseptic concepts like a balanced budget but a private embrace of the Religious Right — only makes this point clearer.

Some theoretical ways out of this quandary can be extracted from existing research, particularly by geographers. A group of scholars has, for different reasons and for some time now, challenged the notion of an omnipresent neoliberalism. They have not been reacting specifically to the question of neoliberalism's death — in most cases they are trying in fact to cope with its apparent omnipresence — but their insights can be meaningfully adapted to the purpose of scrutinizing neoliberalism's putative demise. First, some scholars have challenged omnipresent neoliberalism on geographical grounds. They argue that localities filter and define neoliberalism at least as much as they (localities) are filtered and defined by such ideas (Mitchell 2001; Brenner and Theodore 2002; Keil 2002; D. Wilson 2004). Within this conception, neoliberalism is simply part of a local-global dialectic, rather than a top-down set of processes. As David Wilson explains,

> This political project [neoliberalism] is anything but a "top-down" brute and desensitized imposition on cities. I believe it is best conceptualized as a series of differentiated, keenly negotiating, processural, and space-mobilizing constructions in new political and economic times. These governances, in general principle, are outgrowths of new economic times and circumstances. But they are constituted and re-constituted through the vagaries of the situated: social hierarchies, situated knowledges, meanings, and politics define contemporary problems, villains, victims, salvationists, solutions, and programmatic responses. (2004, 780)

As evidence for this standpoint, authors in this school often refer to ways that local variations of neoliberalism challenge the wider meaning of the concept as set forth by its proponents like Hayek and Friedman. They argue that, as such, we should view neoliberalism as a locally contingent process rather than a pure, ideal type that simply lands in different localities.

A second group of scholars has challenged the internal consistency of neoliberalism itself. Even if it is omnipresent, they argue, it is so varied that it does not result in a singular message. Jamie Gough (2002) and Neil Brenner and Nik Theodore (2002), for example, have suggested that neoliberalism entails a form of state intervention that contradicts one of its own basic premises: that of the minimalist state (see also Polanyi 1944). As such, any attempt to implement such a vision is afflicted with a basic contradiction: in order to enact a minimalist state environment, direct interventions by the state are necessary. John Gray (1989) has taken a different tack, challenging the internal consistency of the neoliberal project by questioning whether liberalism itself is coherent enough to be considered a singular idea. He cites numerous examples of canonical "liberal" thinkers who fundamentally contradict the work of their predecessors. Seen as a larger project, he argues, there are few if any foundational ideas that all liberals would use when defining themselves.

Third, a school of thought has challenged omnipresent neoliberalism by arguing that the term "neoliberalism" is used to encapsulate a set of processes that are either so different or so loosely connected to the liberal project that they have rendered the term meaninglessly broad (Isin 1998; Larner 2000, 2003; D. Wilson 2004). "Neoliberalism" is often used, for example, to cover all things related to business (see Gough 2002 for a critique of this) or all things related to the Right, when—even if seen as intellectually coherent—it actually represents a much narrower set of ideas. One reason that the term is so meaninglessly broad, according to this line of thought, is that it elides a set of governing practices (governmentality) that cannot be usefully encapsulated by the neoliberal metanarrative. Wendy Larner recently lamented that "in these accounts of neoliberalism, for all their geographical and scalar diversity, little attention is paid to the *different variants* of neoliberalism, to the *hybrid nature* of contemporary policies and programmes, or to the *multiple and contradictory aspects* of neoliberal spaces, techniques, and subjects" (2003, 509, emphasis in original). She and other social scientists are worried about this turn of events because they believe it leads to political strategies that are equipped only to combat broad-based ideological forces but are ill-equipped to combat the highly local forms of neoliberalism that actually exist.

For these and other reasons, scholars have increasingly chosen to frame neoliberalism as an "actually existing," locally contingent process (Mitchell 2001; Brenner and Theodore 2002; D. Wilson 2004), or at least as something that needs to be seen in historical segments (Peck and Tickell 2002). The reasons for emphasizing contingency are as varied as the intellectual strategies used to make these arguments. One reason for this, largely following from

Foucault and Derrida, is rooted in concerns about the construction of language in relation to its empirical referent. Many are concerned that the seemingly omnipresent nature of neoliberalism hides the discursively constructed nature of the ideology. Others are concerned politically with the discursive portrayal of a concept that is monolithic, omnipresent, and therefore largely impossible to contest. Following in part from J. K. Gibson-Graham's (1996) work, such authors are concerned that ideal-type neoliberalism is politically debilitating to the Left because it backgrounds the fissures and contradictions (both internal and external) to the "project." A third concern is rooted in the fact that much of the literature on contingent neoliberalism is derived from the discipline of geography, which has long been characterized by a tension between nomothetic spatial law development and an idiographic concern for the power of individual places. Recent developments in geography—particularly postmodern geography—have persuaded many that it is analytically and politically misguided to seek out placeless metanarratives to explain localities (Gregory 1996; Dear and Flusty 1998), though it should be noted that this viewpoint is far from unanimous in the wider urban studies literature. In any case, the intellectual support for contingent neoliberalism is both extensive in scope and deeply rooted in several well-developed schools of thought.

But it is ultimately a fourth group of scholars that I want to highlight here, because they illuminate the partiality of neoliberalism without either diminishing its importance (this is, I think, the weakness of the aforementioned groups) or engaging in the fallacy of assuming that the language of critical scholars is the primary driving force behind its power. This school of thought challenges the emphasis on neoliberalism within cities given the presence of other, parallel processes and ideologies—in other words, it emphasizes the notion that neoliberalism is partial. Robert Jessop (2002), in particular, has argued that the analytical emphasis on neoliberalism as an omnipresent force elides the presence of other forces that are transforming cities, such as neocorporatism, neocommunitarianism, and neostatism. As Jessop explains,

> Liberalism is a complex, multifaceted phenomenon. It is: a polyvalent conceptual ensemble in economic, political, and ideological *discourse*; a strongly contested *strategic concept* for restructuring market-state relations with many disputes over its scope, application, and limitations; and a recurrent yet historically variable pattern of economic, political, and social *organization* in modern societies. Liberalism rarely, if ever, exists in pure form; it typically coexists with elements from other discourses, strategies, and organizational patterns. (2002, 549, emphasis in original)

In short, the fact that neoliberalism is a dominant force should not lead us to the conclusion that it is the *only* force. Parallel processes and ideas challenge, morph, and sometimes blatantly contradict a purely neoliberal project.

A PARTIAL CONCLUSION

Is religious neoliberalism extinct? It ultimately depends on what we mean by neoliberalism, religion, and extinction. If we mean that religious neoliberalism has been challenged, perhaps seriously, by recent events and that it will cease to be the singular guiding principle that it has been for the past thirty years, then *perhaps* we can offer a qualified yes. If we mean, however, that the core ideas of religious neoliberalism, its ideational supports, especially the religious ones, are literally dead, then we can offer an unqualified no. Neoliberalism, religious or not, has always been, and continues to be, partial. Even during its high-water marks during the last three decades, there were always countervailing forces that contradicted it, challenged it, paralleled it, and provided resistance to it.

But by the same token, saying that religious neoliberalism is partial is not to say that it was or is unimportant. Its central ideas of individualism, market reliance, property rights, and small government, justified by a curiously literal reading of the Bible, are in many ways threads borrowed from the larger liberal project—particularly in North America. It was neither as alive as many framed it to be during the late twentieth century nor as dead as some are framing it to be now. It is a reminder that the American Right is a great deal more complicated than many of its observers have characterized it to be and that the pre-2006 electoral success of the Republican Party would suggest. The Right is composed of multiple threads and motivations. Religious neoliberalism has been a conscious effort to fuse together two of those threads. It was ultimately unsuccessful (so far, at least), but the component parts remain. Faith in the market, faith in the individual, and faith in small (or nonexistent) government continue to exist and will undoubtedly be reconstituted in the future. Religious neoliberalism may not be the commonsense ideology it once was, but the echoes of its core principles remain crucial to understanding the American political landscape in the coming decades.

NOTES

INTRODUCTION. A FORCE FOR GOOD GREATER THAN GOVERNMENT

1. Under the Bush administration, the office was titled the "White House Office of Faith-Based and Community Initiatives."

CHAPTER ONE. FAITH, WELFARE, AND NEOLIBERALISM

1. The *New York Times* and the *Wall Street Journal* collaborated on a poll that described the demographics and politics of Tea Partiers (*New York Times* 2010).

2. It should also be noted that both Bush and Gore were completely amenable to the larger trend of which the funding of religious charities was a part, namely, the contracting of social service provision to nonprofits. This has been the prevailing pattern of social welfare in the United States since the 1960s. Much, though not all, of the emphasis of this funding has been toward community-based providers.

3. Green (2005) defines "movement politics" as challenges to existing political institutions, "quiescent politics" as the detachment from political institutions, and "regularized politics" as the adaptation to established political institutions. The Scopes trial, famously portrayed in the film *Inherit the Wind*, involved a teacher in Tennessee in the 1920s, John Scopes, who taught evolution in his science class, in defiance of a law that forbade the teaching of any theory that denied divine creation. Though Scopes lost, the trial had the effect of marginalizing the evangelical community as anti-intellectual.

4. As Hammack notes in his review of the book, Olasky's *Tragedy of American Compassion* was not reviewed by a single mainstream academic journal upon its release in 1992. Most considered it to be not scholarship, he goes on to argue, but a thinly veiled, poorly researched polemic (Hammack 1996). It is true, however, that while Olasky's book has not inspired mainstream academics, it has certainly inspired a group of nonacademic clergy like Rod Parsley (2006) to write books that enthusiastically support Olasky's contentions.

5. In one particularly acerbic critique, Massing suggests that "in its own way, *The Tragedy of American Compassion* is an illuminating book. The spectacle of its author sitting in his air-conditioned aerie at the Heritage Foundation while condemning soup kitchens for handing out too much food shows just how corrupt our notion of compassion has become" (1992,60).

6. The conservative *Washington Times* ran a story titled "100-year-old-idea inspires proposals to revamp welfare," in which the author argued that the pluralism inherent

in "sphere sovereignty" was a useful model that the United States could use in trying to wed secular welfare ideas with sectarian providers.

7. Olasky was responsible for the now-famous language of "compassionate conservatism" during the presidential run, outlining the philosophy in a book of the same title (Olasky 2000).

8. In one such example, the Obama Justice Department did not unambiguously strike down the Bush administration's allowance of employment discrimination (on the basis of religion) by faith-based organizations. Instead, Obama's Faith-Based and Neighborhood Partnerships director, Joshua DuBois, stated that the administration would evaluate such claims on a "case-by-case" basis (*Los Angeles Times* 2009; Fingerhut 2009).

9. For more on this argument, see Clarkson (2009); of particular relevance is the essay by Osagyefo Sekou (2009).

10. For more on this variant, see Hackworth (2009a, 2010b).

CHAPTER TWO. RELIGIOUS NEOLIBERALISM(S)

1. Ironically, given the importance of this perspective for radical conservatives, these verses have also been used more recently to advocate a more progressive stance toward the environment (Cizik 2005).

2. The difference, of course, between Kuyper's vision and that promoted by Dominionists, is that Kuyper, while himself a Christian, felt that the same "sovereignty" should be granted to churches and secular groups alike.

3. North was actually somewhat insecure about his level of productivity vis-à-vis his late father-in-law, Rushdoony. North once quipped that he struggled to maintain the standard that Rushdoony set: "Rushdoony is the Marx of this movement. I'm trying very hard to be the Engels" (Diamond 1989, 136).

4. North has a PhD in economics from the University of California, Riverside, awarded in 1967.

5. Rudin (2006) has suggested that the term "Christocrats" be used instead, though I doubt that this would allay the concerns of those who object to the term "Dominionist."

6. Among the most common users of this passage are North American conservatives, after Reagan and Mulroney (the Canadian prime minister in the 1980s), who aimed to weave a "small government" narrative with a moralizing one.

7. Rothbard is actually an anarcho-libertarian, a group with which many Christian libertarians disagree wholeheartedly.

8. An interesting sidebar to this notion of personal wealth as a gift from God is that even Jim Bakker himself repudiated the idea as bogus as he was being carted off to prison for fraud.

9. "Church" may be a bit of a misnomer as his congregation is so large that it fully occupies a former professional basketball arena (previously known as the Compaq Center).

CHAPTER THREE. COMPASSIONATE NEOLIBERALISM?

1. See, for example, National Association of Evangelicals Archive, 1958a, 1958b, 1960, 1961, 1962, 1963, 1965, 1973a, 1973b, 1982, and 1988.

2. For an example of a short resolution, see National Association of Evangelicals Archive 1958b. For a lengthier resolution, see National Association of Evangelicals Archive, 2004.

3. It should be noted, however, that *Christianity Today* is not the most widely read evangelical magazine but arguably the most mainstream (which is why it was selected for the research here).

4. Only substantive references were retained in the database. "Substantive" was defined as containing at least one full sentence referring to an actual example of or the general concept of welfare.

CHAPTER FOUR. MAINSTREAM JESUS ECONOMICS

1. Focus on "branding" has become a mild obsession for the organization. As one Habitat official interviewed for this study boasted, "[Our brand value is] somewhere between McDonalds and Starbucks."

2. Habitat Los Angeles, for example, receives roughly one hundred applications for every house it is able to build, according to an interview conducted as part of this study. Habitat New York City received over five thousand requests for applications in 2006 and was able to eventually build forty-one homes (also according to an interview). Rates in smaller cities and rural areas are similarly low. In Omaha, Nebraska, 500–600 people request applications, 160 complete them, and twenty houses are eventually built (Habitat Omaha 2007). Canadian figures are similarly low. In Toronto, approximately 100 potential clients take applications, 10 complete them, with 1 eventually resulting in a home, according to an official with knowledge of Toronto Habitat. In Vancouver, British Columbia, the Habitat affiliate receives twenty to thirty inquiries a week, approximately 50 percent of which are eliminated due to some criterion (usually income being too low). Every few years, about 300 prescreened families are invited to an information session about going further in the process, about 20 to 30 percent (60–90 families) of whom then fill out formal applications, which result in about 4 families receiving homes.

3. I define "manifest" and "latent" content analyses as two ends of a spectrum. Manifest analyses are more systematic, less interpretative, and often more quantitative than latent (or discourse) analyses. Latent analyses are more interpretive, qualitative, and contextual. In practice, all content analyses contain elements of interpretation, and there are a variety of ways to interpret texts—this study is no different in that respect.

Habitat for Humanity opened its first affiliate in 1976 in the United States, so I searched for articles that went back as close to this date as possible. Habitat for Humanity Canada, however, did not open its first affiliate until 1985, in Winkler, Manitoba, so the

Canadian search went back to that date. The searches were completed in June 2008, but given that 2008 was not yet a full year, articles from that year were read but omitted from the quantitative analysis.

4. Articles from the *New York Times* were obtained through Factiva for the period 1980–2007, and by Proquest for the period 1976–80. Articles from the *Wall Street Journal* were obtained through Factiva for the period 1979–2007, and by print index volumes of the *Wall Street Journal* for the years 1976–79. The *Washington Times* was established in 1982. Articles from the *Washington Times* were obtained through Factiva for the period 1988–2008. I was unable to gain access to the *Washington Times* archives for the period 1982–88. Articles from the *Globe and Mail* were obtained from Factiva for the period 1985–2007. The *National Post* was established in 1998; it absorbed the existing *Financial Post* (which dates back to 1907). Articles after 1998 were thus found under "*National Post*" while pre-1998 articles were found under "*Financial Post*." Articles for this publication (*National/Financial Post*) were obtained from Factiva for the period 1998–2007 and from Proquest for the period 1985–98. Articles from the *Toronto Star* were obtained from Factiva for the periods 1985–2002 and 2004–7. For reasons that are unclear, Factiva did not have access to *Toronto Star* articles for 2003, so Proquest was used for that year.

5. To ensure that included articles focused on Habitat for Humanity, only those with the following criteria were retained: (1) "Habitat" in the title *and* the text; or (2) at least one full sentence in the text that was about some aspect of the organization. This eliminated many articles in which Habitat for Humanity was mentioned only incidentally. Some of the more common forms of eliminated incidental references included (1) wedding announcements in which Habitat was mentioned as an organization for which the bride or groom had volunteered; (2) announcements of events where Habitat was mentioned only incidentally (references such as, "a benefit was held for Habitat" [with no other information] were omitted, while references like "Habitat, which renovates housing in Bridgeport and [has enlisted] volunteers since 1993" were retained); (3) any repeats or very close pieces within the same newspaper; (4) photo captions that were not attached to a larger article that discussed Habitat; (5) corrections of previous articles; and (6) advertisements for ReStore, a chain of building-supplies thrift shops managed by Habitat Canada (some references were kept if substantive mention of Habitat for Humanity occurred later in the text, but most of these were regularly repeated classified ads).

6. Though such moments generated greater media attention for NGOs like Habitat, there was no discernible long-term influence on the coverage.

7. The term "local managerialist state" is derived from Harvey's (1989) conceptualization of municipal governance under Keynesianism. It is used here to refer to government actions that are managerialist in nature—e.g., imposing and enforcing building regulations—and is contrasted with the "entrepreneurial state," which is much more accommodating for business interests.

8. These instances were counted in the quantitative portion of this study only if the

statement by the Habitat official was not counterbalanced or challenged by the journalist elsewhere in the article.

9. In cases when a counterargument was offered, the article was not coded as having presented a direct alternative to "government failure."

10. A chi-square analysis comparing newspapers across the dimension of national origin (Canadian newspapers versus American newspapers) was also performed. In all scenarios that were run, no significant differences were found between the coverage in the two countries (see Hackworth 2009b for more detail).

CHAPTER FIVE. PRACTICING RELIGIOUS NEOLIBERALISM

1. Among the critics were a group of clergy and scholars who formed the group Theocracy Watch (http://theocracywatch.org/).

2. "Faith-saturated" organizations are those in which there is no meaningful distinction between their efforts to proselytize and their efforts to provide social services.

3. These figures were obtained as follows. To derive an estimate of total rescue mission beds, I divided AGRM's most recent figure of 15,495,197 bed-nights in 2006 by 365 to arrive at 42,452.5. To derive a percentage of U.S. emergency shelter total, I then divided this figure by the Department of Housing and Urban Development's (2008) most recent counts of 211,451 emergency shelter beds and 211,205 transitional housing beds in 2006–7, to arrive at 20.1 percent and 10.0 percent, respectively.

4. There are, of course, homeless shelters that profess other variants of Christianity (especially Catholic shelters) and facilities that serve under the banner of different faiths (e.g., Judaism, Islam) altogether. But "gospel rescue mission" refers exclusively to a fairly fundamentalist variant of Protestant evangelical Christianity.

5. Like other homeless shelters and their staff (DeVerteuil 2006), gospel rescue missions cannot be distilled to a singular omnipresent theme or motivation. But the approach described here is the prevailing pole toward which the gospel rescue mission approach and the identity of its volunteers gravitate.

6. The majority (70.1 percent) of the 284 member missions had some form of e-mail contact available. Seventy-five rescue missions (26.4 percent) were reachable only through online text boxes managed by the AGRM or the webmaster of the rescue mission website, while 10 missions (3.5 percent) had no contact information at all. These distinctions are worth noting, not least because they indicate differing probabilities of reply to the survey. That is, direct e-mails to individuals associated with a given rescue mission are more likely to be answered than indirect contact attempts (e.g., via info@rescuemission.org) or text-box messages sent to unspecified persons in the mission. This likely contributed to a probable bias toward larger, more technologically sophisticated missions and probably led to an underrepresentation of smaller, less well funded rescue missions. This, of course, does not disqualify the results but is worth noting to show that this sample, while large, is slightly skewed toward larger, more prosperous rescue missions.

7. The survey questions and e-mail reminders were written by the author. An attempt was made, when possible, to solicit the viewpoint of the highest official within the rescue mission (most often the executive director), but responses from knowledgeable staff were also accepted. In each survey, confidentiality was assured, and the web-based software used ensured that it was maintained.

8. Thirty-one respondents also wrote in "thrift stores," which was not included as a preset option.

9. This figure includes only *sheltered* point-in-time counts done by HUD and local officials. They are considered more reliable than *unsheltered* point-in-time counts, which are plagued by problems, not the least of which is the great deal of local uncertainty about who counts as homeless under the Bush administration's more stringent rules, which emphasize only the "chronically" homeless (Del Casino and Jocoy 2008).

10. This figure does not separate transitional and emergency shelters, as the HUD data do not facilitate such a separation. However, it is probable that rescue missions contribute more emergency shelter beds than transitional beds (only the Bowery Mission provides the latter).

CHAPTER SIX. RELIGIOUS NEOLIBERALISM AS DEFAULT

1. It should be noted that the phrase "act of God" and general invocations of the divine significantly predate the present context as a way to absolve corporations (i.e., insurance disclaimers) and governments from responsibility for "natural" disasters. This section is intended only to highlight their frequency in the aftermath of Katrina, not to suggest that such invocations are completely novel.

2. Robertson's Operation Blessing has also been accused of being a vehicle for possibly illegal work in Africa and a way to personally enrich Robertson (see Blumenthal 2005 for more on this organization).

3. These approaches are identified as "quasi-Calvinist" to convey the embedded tendencies within Habitat for Humanity and the New Orleans Rescue Mission (both evangelically oriented) to espouse Calvinist precepts such as "sovereign grace" and "total depravity." Such beliefs both influence client selection and reflect a Calvinist-infused "common sense" within these organizations that intersects with particular conceptions of the market operating within neoliberalism.

CHAPTER SEVEN. END TIMES FOR RELIGIOUS NEOLIBERALISM?

1. Cizik eventually lost his job at the NAE in part because of his unpopular political stances.

2. As evidence for his assertion, Sager echoes Kuo's (2006) argument that far less money has been allocated to the program than previously promised and that it was largely used as a tool to garner African American votes.

REFERENCES

Allbaugh, J. (2001). Testimony before the Veterans Affairs, Housing and Urban Development and Independent Agencies Subcommittee of the Senate Appropriations Committee, May 16, 2001. *Federal Emergency Management Website (online).* http://www.fema.gov/about/director/allbaugh/testimony/051601.shtm. (Accessed October 2009).

Acton Institute. (2008). About the Acton Institute. *Acton Institute website (online).* http://www.acton.org/about/index.php. (Accessed October 2008).

Acton, J. E. E. D. (1988). *Essays in religion, politics, and morality.* Ed. J. R. Fears. Vol. 3 of *Selected writings of Lord Acton.* Indianapolis: Liberty Classics.

AGRM (Association of Gospel Rescue Missions). (2006). Services provided to the homeless and needy in 2006. *AGRM website (online).* http://www.agrm.org/statistics/06-stats.html. (Accessed September 2008).

———. (2008). *AGRM website (online).* http://www.agrm.org. (Accessed September 2008).

Alcorn, R. (1989). *Money, possessions and eternity.* Wheaton, Ill.: Tyndale House.

Anderson, P. (2000). Renewals. *New Left Review, 1*(January/February), 1–18.

Antle, W. J. (2007). Evangelicals and the state: A law professor makes a case for a libertarian Christianity. *Reason Magazine* (June) *(online).* http://www.reason.com/news/show/119726.html. (Accessed October 2008).

Aron, L., & Sharkey, P. (2002). *The 1996 national survey of homeless assistance providers and clients faith-based and secular non-profit programs.* Washington D.C.: Urban Institute. Research report.

AUSCS (Americans United for the Separation of Church and State). (n.d.). The "Faith-Based" Initiative: churches, social services and your tax dollars. *Faith and Freedom Series (online).* http://www.au.org/site/PageServer?pagename=issues_faithbased. (Accessed March 2007).

Baggett, J. P. (2001). *Habitat for Humanity: Building private homes, building public religion.* Philadelphia: Temple University Press.

Balko, R. (2005). When the catastrophe is government. *Fox News website* (September 7) *(online).* http://www.cato.org/pub_display.php?pub_id=4659. (Accessed May 2009).

Bandow, D. (1994). *The politics of envy: Statism as theology.* New Brunswick, N.J.: Transaction.

———. (2005). Break up Congress. *American Spectator website* (September 30) *(online)*. http://www.cato.org/pub_display.php?pub_id=5113. (Accessed May 2009).

Barbieux, K. (2008). Thoughts on the Bible. *(Online)*. http://thehomelessguy.wordpress.com/2008/02/09/thoughts-on-the-bible/. (Accessed August 2008).

Beaumont, J. (2004). Workfare, associationism and the "underclass" in the United States: Contrasting faith-based action on urban poverty in a liberal welfare regime. In H. Noordegraaf & R. Volz (Eds.), *Churches and diaconal institutions in Europe against poverty: Social exclusion and social actions* (pp. 249–78). Bochum: SWI Press.

———. (2008). Faith action on urban social issues. *Urban Studies, 45*(10), 2019–34.

Beaumont, J., & Dias, C. (2008). Faith-based organizations and urban social justice in the Netherlands. *Tijdschrift voor Economische en Sociale Geografie, 99*(4), 382–92.

Bigelow, G. (2005). Let there be markets: The evangelical roots of economics. *Harper's Magazine, 310*(1860), 33–38.

Black, A. E., Koopman, D. L., & Ryden, D. K. (2004). *Of little faith: The politics of George W. Bush's faith-based initiatives*. Washington, D.C.: Georgetown University Press.

Blumenthal, M. (2005). Pat Robertson's Katrina cash. *The Nation*. September 7.

Boaz, D. (2005). Franklin Delano Bush. *CATO website* (September 29) *(online)*. http://www.cato.org/pub_display.php?pub_id=5071. (Accessed May 2009).

Boleyn-Fitzgerald, P. (1999). Misfortune, welfare reform, and right-wing egalitarianism. *Critical Review, 13*(1/2), 141–63.

Bonner, A. (2002). *Enacted Christianity: Evangelical rescue missions in the United States and Canada*. Philadelphia: Xlibris.

Boston Globe. (2005). Bush rallies faith-based groups, charities for aid. September 7. (Milligan, S.).

Box, R. (1999). Running government like a business: Implications for public administration theory and practice. *American Review of Public Administration, 29*(1), 19–43.

Brenner, N., & Theodore, N. (2002). Cities and the geographies of "actually existing" neoliberalism. *Antipode, 34*(3), 349–79.

Briggs, X. de Souza. (2004). Faith and mortar: Religious organizations and affordable housing strategy in urban America. In R. Anglin (Ed.), *Building the organizations that build communities* (pp. 1–9). Washington, D.C.: HUD.

Brown, M. (2005). Testimony before the House select bipartisan committee. In *Investigation of the Federal Emergency Management Agency's preparation for and response to Hurricane Katrina*. September 27.

Brown, W. (2006). American nightmare: Neoliberalism, neoconservatism, and de-democratization. *Political Theory, 34*(6), 690–714.

Burns, J. (2009). *Goddess of the market: Ayn Rand and the American right*. Oxford: Oxford University Press.

Burt, M. R., Aron, L. Y., Douglas, T., Valente, J., Lee, E., & Iwen, B. (1999).

Homelessness: Programs and the people they serve; Findings of the national survey of homeless assistance providers and clients. Washington, D.C.: Urban Institute. Research report.

Casanova, J. (1994). *Public religions in the modern world*. Chicago: University of Chicago Press.

Chang, H. (1997). The economics and politics of regulation. *Cambridge Journal of Economics, 21*(6), 703–28.

Chaves, M. (2001a). Going on faith: Six myths about faith-based initiatives. *Christian Century, 118*(25), 20–23.

———. (2001b). Religious congregations and welfare reform. *Society, 38*(2), 21–27.

———. (2001c). The newer deal: Social work and religion in partnership. *Sociology Of Religion, 62*(1), 132–33.

Christianity Today. (2009). *Readership report (online)*. http://www.cti-advertising.com/files/publicationfiles/ChristianityTodayrev03_09.pdf. (Accessed July 2009).

City of Nashville (2004). The strategic framework for ending chronic homelessness in Nashville. *City of Nashville website (online)*. http://www.ich.gov/slocal/plans/nashville.pdf. (Accessed July 2009).

Cizik, R. (2005). A history of the public policy resolutions of the National Association of Evangelicals. In R. Sider & D. Knippers (Eds.), *Toward an evangelical public policy: Political strategies for the health of a nation* (pp. 35–63). Grand Rapids, Mich.: Baker Books.

Clarkson, F. (1994). Theocratic Dominionism gains influence. *Public Eye* (May/June) *(online)*. http://www.publiceye.org/magazine/v08n1/chrisre1.html. (Accessed October 2008).

———. (Ed.). (2009). *Dispatches from the Religious Left*. New York: IG Publishing.

Clauson, M. (2006). *A history of the idea of "God's law" (theonomy): Its origins, development and place in political and legal thought*. Lewiston, N.Y.: Edwin Mellon Press.

Cnaan, R. A., Boddie, S. C., Handy, F., Yancey, G., & Schneider, R. (2002). *The invisible caring hand: American congregations and the provision of welfare*. New York: New York University Press.

Cnaan, R., Boddie, S., McGrew, C., & Kang, J. (2006). *The other Philadelphia story: How local congregations support quality of life in urban America*. Philadelphia: University of Pennsylvania Press.

Cnaan, R. A., Boddie, S. C., & Wineburg, R. J. (1999). *The Newer Deal: Social work and religion in partnership*. New York: Columbia University Press.

Coalition for the Homeless. (n.d.). Ensuring the right to shelter: The first court decision in *Callahan v. Carey* requiring the provision of shelter for homeless men in New York City. *COH website (online)*. http://www.coalitionforthehomeless.org/Page.asp?ID=421. (Accessed July 2009).

Colson, C., & Morse, A. (2009). Protecting our little platoons: There's reason to be concerned for the future of voluntary organizations. *Christianity Today, 53*(6), 64.

Connolly, W. (2005). The evangelical-capitalist resonance machine. *Political Theory, 33*(6), 869–86.

———. (2008). *Capitalism and Christianity, American style*. Durham, N.C.: Duke University Press.

Conradson, D. (2008). Expressions of charity and action towards justice: Faith-based welfare provision in urban New Zealand. *Urban Studies, 45*(10), 2117–41.

Contemporary Authors Online. (2008a). *Joel Osteen*. Thomson Gale.

———. (2008b). *T. D. Jakes*. Thomson Gale.

Crowe, S. (1981). Reducing poverty: Christians debate government's role; Sider and North spar over issue at Gordon-Conwell Seminary. *Christianity Today, 25*(9).

Daly, L. (2006). *God and the welfare state*. Boston: MIT Press.

Davis, M. (2005). The predators of New Orleans. *Le Monde Diplomatique*. October 2, 2005.

Dawson, J. (1957). The Christian view of the welfare state. *Christianity Today, 1*(9), 3–5.

Dear, M., & Flusty, S. (1998). Postmodern urbanism. *Annals of the Association of American Geographers, 88*(1), 50–72.

Del Casino, V. J., & Jocoy, C. (2008). Neoliberal subjectivities, the "new" homelessness, and struggles over spaces of/in the city. *Antipode, 40*(2), 192–99.

DeVerteuil, G. (2006). The local state and homeless shelters: Beyond revanchism? *Cities, 23*(2), 109–20.

De Vita, C., Kramer, F., Eyster, L., Hall, S., Kehayova, P., & Triple, T. (2008). *The role of faith-based and community organizations in post-Katrina human service relief efforts*. Washington, D.C.: The Urban Institute.

Diamond, S. (1989). *Spiritual warfare: The politics of the Christian right*. Boston: South End Press.

———. (1995). *Roads to dominion: Right-winged movements and political power in the United States*. New York: Guilford.

———. (1998). *Not by politics alone: The enduring influence of the Christian right*. New York: Guilford.

Dilulio, J. J. (2004). Getting faith-based programs right. *Public Interest, 155*(Spring), 75–88.

Dolgoff, R. (1999). What does social welfare produce? *International Social Work, 42*(3), 295–307.

Dumenil, G., & Levy, D. (2004). *Capital resurgent: Roots of the neoliberal revolution*. Cambridge, Mass.: Harvard University Press.

Ebaugh, H. R., Chafetz, J. S., & Pipes, P. F. (2006). The influence of evangelicalism on government funding of faith-based social service organizations. *Review of Religious Research, 47*(4), 380–92.

Edwards, C. (2005). Privatize the Army Corps of Engineers. *Tax & Budget Bulletin No. 27*. Washington, D.C.: CATO Institute.

Elisha, O. (2008). Moral ambitions of grace: The paradox of compassion and accountability in evangelical faith-based activism. *Cultural Anthropology, 23*(1), 154–89.

Fagan, R. (1986a) Modern rescue missions: A survey of the International Union of Gospel Missions. *Journal of Drug Issues, 16*(4), 495–509.

———. (1986b). Ministering in the hinterland: A survey of rescue mission directors. *Journal of Pastoral Counseling, 11*, 79–87.

———. (1987). Skid row missions: A religious approach to alcoholism. *Journal of Religion and Health, 26*(2), 153–71.

———. (1998). Religious nonprofit organizations: An examination of rescue missions and the homeless. *Social Thought, 18*(4), 21–48.

Fagnoni, C. (2005). Testimony before the Subcommittee on Oversight. *Hurricanes Katrina and Rita: Provision of charitable assistance*. Committee on Ways and Means, House of Representatives. December 13, 2005.

Falwell, J. (1980). *Listen, America!* Garden City, N.Y: Doubleday.

FEMA (Federal Emergency Management Administration). (2005). Cash sought to help hurricane victims, volunteers should not self-dispatch. *Press Release HQ-05-117*. August 29.

Fingerhut, E. (2009). Obama upholds case-by-case approach on religious hiring. The Global News Service of the Jewish People. (April 20) *(online)*. http://www.jta.org/news/article/2009/04/20/1004500/obama-believes-case-by-case-is-right-way-on-faith-based-legal-issues. (Accessed July 2011).

Friedman, M., with R. Friedman. (1962). *Capitalism and freedom*. Chicago: University of Chicago Press.

Frye, G. (1996). *If I were a carpenter: Twenty years of Habitat for Humanity*. Winston-Salem, N.C.: J. F. Blair.

Fuller, M. (2006). Habitat for Humanity and the Peachtree Presbyterian Church. In J. S. Shook (Ed.), *Making housing happen: Faith-based affordable housing models* (pp. 45–55). St. Louis: Chalice Press.

Fuller, M., & Scott, D. (1980). *Love in the mortar joints: The story of Habitat for Humanity*. New Jersey: Association Press, New Century.

GAO (Government Accountability Office). (2006). *Faith-Based and Community Initiative: Improvements in monitoring grantees and measuring performance could enhance accountability*. Report to Congressional Requesters. Washington, D.C.: GAO.

Gibson-Graham, J. K. (1996). *The end of capitalism (as we knew it): A feminist critique of political economy*. Oxford: Blackwell.

Giri, A. K. (2002). *Building in the margins of shacks: A vision and projects for Habitat for Humanity*. Hyderabad, India: Orient Longman.

Girvetz, H. (1963). *The evolution of liberalism*. New York: Collier.

Globe and Mail. (2004). Habitat for Humanity builds more than houses. July 30. (Parsons, M.).

———. (2005). Habitat home is "like winning jackpot." September 26. (Appleby, T.).

Goldsmith, S., Eimicke, W., & Torres, M. (2006). *The role of faith organizations in affordable housing*. Cambridge, Mass.: JFK School of Government, Harvard. Research report.

Goonewardena, K. (2003). The future of planning at the "end of history." *Planning Theory, 2*(3), 183–224.

Gotham, K. F., & Greenburg, M. (2008). From 9/11 to 8/29: Post-disaster recovery and rebuilding in New York and New Orleans. *Social Forces, 87*(2), 1039–62.

Gough, J. (2002). Neoliberalism and socialisation in the contemporary city: Opposites, complements and instabilities. *Antipode, 34*(3), 405–26.

Grace, M. F., & Klein, R. W. (2007). Facing Mother Nature. *Regulation* (Fall), 28–34.

Grann, D. (1999). Where W. got compassion. *New York Times Magazine*. September 12.

Gray, J. (1989). *Liberalisms*. London: Routledge.

Green, J. (2005). Seeking a place: Evangelical Protestants and public engagement in the twentieth century. In R. Sider & D. Knippers (Eds.), *Toward an evangelical public policy: Political strategies for the health of a nation* (pp. 35–63). Grand Rapids, Mich.: Baker Books.

Gregory, D. (1996). Areal differentiation and post-modern human geography. In J. Agnew, D. Livingstone, & A. Rogers (Eds.), *Human geography: An essential anthology*. Oxford: Blackwell.

Gruber, J., & Hungerman, D. (2007). Faith-based charity and crowd-out during the Great Depression. *Journal of Public Economics, 91*(5/6), 1043–69.

Habitat for Humanity International. (2008). *Habitat for Humanity International Website (online)*. http://www.habitat.org/. (Accessed July 8, 2008).

Habitat Omaha. (2007). *Habitat for Humanity Omaha Website (online)*. http://www.habitatomaha.org/. (Accessed July 20, 2007).

Hackworth, J. (2002). Local autonomy, bond-rating agencies and neoliberal urbanism in the U.S. *International Journal of Urban and Regional Research, 26*(4), 707–25.

———. (2003). Public housing and the re-scaling of regulation in the U.S. *Environment and Planning A*, 35(3), 531–49.

———. (2007). *The neoliberal city: Governance, ideology, and development in American urbanism*. Ithaca, N.Y.: Cornell University Press.

———. (2008). The durability of roll-out neoliberalism under centre-left governance: The case of Ontario's social housing sector. *Studies in Political Economy, 81*(Spring), 7–26.

———. (2009a). Neoliberalism, partiality and the politics of faith-based welfare in the United States. *Studies in Political Economy 84*, 155–80.

———. (2009b). Normalizing "solutions" to "government failure": Media representations of Habitat for Humanity. *Environment and Planning A, 41*(11), 2686–2705.

———. (2010a). Compassionate neoliberalism?: Evangelical Christianity, the welfare state, and the politics of the Right. *Studies in Political Economy 86*, 83-108.

———. (2010b). Faith, welfare, and the city: The mobilization of religious organizations for neoliberal ends. *Urban Geography 31*(6).

Hackworth, J., & Moriah, A. (2006). Neoliberalism, contingency, and urban policy: The case of social housing in Ontario. *International Journal of Urban and Regional Research, 30*(3), 510–27.

Hagerty, B. (2006). Evangelical leaders urge action on climate change. *National Public Radio* (February 8) *(online)*. http://www.npr.org/templates/story/story.php?storyId=5194527. (Accessed March 2007).

Hammack, D. (1996). Review of The Tragedy of American Compassion 1995 edition, by Marvin Olasky. *Nonprofit and Voluntary Sector Quarterly*, 25(2), 259–68.

Harper, J. (2006). Ideology and critical infrastructure protection. *CATO Website* (December 4) *(online)*. http://www.cato-at-liberty.org/2006/12/04/ideology-and-critical-infrastructure-protection/. (Accessed May 2009).

Harris, E. (2007). Historical regulation of Victoria's water sector: A case of government failure? *Australian Journal of Agricultural and Resource Economics*, 51(3), 343–52.

Harris, M., Halfpenny, P., & Rochester, C. (2003). A social policy role for faith-based organisations? Lessons from the U.K. Jewish voluntary sector. *Journal of Social Policy*, 32(1), 93–112.

Harvey, D. (1989). From managerialism to entrepreneurialism: The transformation of urban governance in late capitalism. *Geografiska Annaler*, 71, 3–17.

———. (2005). *A brief history of neoliberalism*. Oxford: Oxford University Press.

Hayek, F. (1944). *The road to serfdom*. Chicago: University of Chicago Press.

———. (1960). *The constitution of liberty*. Chicago: University of Chicago Press.

Hays, R. A. (2002). Habitat for Humanity: Building social capital through faith based service. *Journal of Urban Affairs*, 24(3), 247–69.

Hiemstra, J. (2002). Government relations with faith-based non-profit social agencies in Alberta. *Journal of Church and State*, 44(1), 19–44.

Hilfiker, D. (2003). *Urban injustice*. New York: Seven Stories Press.

Hilton, B. (1986). *The age of atonement: The influence of evangelicalism on social and economic thought, 1785–1865*. Oxford: Oxford University Press.

Höpfl, H. (Ed.). (1991). *Luther and Calvin on secular authority*. Cambridge: Cambridge University Press.

HUD (U.S. Department of Housing and Urban Development). (2008). *Third annual homeless assessment report to Congress*. Washington, D.C.: HUD.

Hudson, K., & Coukos, A. (2005). The dark side of the Protestant ethic: A comparative analysis of welfare reform. *Sociological Theory*, 23(1), 1–24.

Hula, R., Jackson-Elmoore, C., & Reese, L. (2007). Mixing God's work and the public business: A framework for the analysis of faith-based service delivery. *Review of Policy Research*, 24(1), 67–89.

Hungerman, D. (2005). Are church and state substitutes? Evidence from the 1996 welfare reform. *Journal of Public Economics*, 89(11/12), 2245–67.

Ignatieff, M. (2005). The broken contract. *New York Times Magazine*. September 25.

Isin, E. (1998). Governing Toronto without government: Liberalism and neoliberalism. *Studies in Political Economy*, 56(Summer), 169–91.

Jackson, R. (1989). Prosperity theology and the faith movement. *Themelios*, 15(1), 16–24.

Jamoul, L., & Wills, J. (2008). Faith in politics. *Urban Studies, 45*(10), 2035–56.

Jeavons, T. (2003). The vitality and independence of religious organizations. *Society*, (January/February), 27–36.

Jessop, R. (2002). Liberalism, neoliberalism, and urban governance: A state-theoretical perspective. *Antipode, 34*(3), 452–72.

Kahl, S. (2005). The religious roots of modern poverty policy: Catholic, Lutheran, and Reformed Protestant traditions compared. *Archives Europeennes de Sociologie, 46*(1), 91–126+171.

Katz, C. (2008). Bad elements: Katrina and the scoured landscape of social reproduction. *Gender, Place and Culture, 15*(1), 15–29.

Kearns, K., Park, C., & Yankoski, L. (2005). Comparing faith-based and secular community service corporations in Pittsburgh and Allegheny County, Pennsylvania. *Nonprofit and Voluntary Sector Quarterly, 34*(2), 206–31.

Keil, R. (2002). "Common-sense" neoliberalism: Progressive conservative urbanism in Toronto, Canada. *Antipode, 34*(3), 578–601.

Kershner, H. (1957). The welfare state: Reply to Dawson. *Christianity Today, 1*(10), 18–19.

Kintz, L. (1997). *Between Jesus and the market: The emotions that matter in right-wing America*. Durham, N.C.: Duke University Press.

———. (2007). Finding the strength to surrender: Marriage, market theocracy, and the spirit of America. *Theory, Culture and Society, 24*(4), 111–30.

Kirkpatrick, D. (2007). The evangelical crack up. *New York Times Magazine*. October 28.

Klein, N. (2007). *Shock doctrine: The rise of disaster capitalism*. Toronto: Random House.

Koelkebeck, T. (2010) Is the religious Right taking over the Tea Party? *Huffington Post* (October 27) *(online)*. http://www.huffingtonpost.com/tim-koelkebeck/post_1153_b_774964.html. (Accessed June 23, 2011).

Kuo, D. (2006). *Tempting faith: An inside story of political seduction*. New York: Free Press.

Kurtz, S. (2005). Dominionist domination. *National Review* (May 2) *(online)*. http://www.nationalreview.com/kurtz/kurtz200505020944.asp. (Accessed October 2008).

Lakewood Church. (2008). About us. *Lakewood Church Website (online)*. http://www.lakewood.cc/AboutUs/NewToLakewood/Pages/NewToLakewood.aspx. (Accessed October 2008).

Larner, W. (2000). Neoliberalism: Policy, ideology, governmentality. *Studies in Political Economy, 63*(Autumn), 5–25.

———. (2003). Neoliberalism? *Environment and planning D, 21*(5), 509–12.

Lee, B. (1989). Stability and change in the urban homeless population. *Demography, 26*(2), 323–34.

Lee, S. (2007). Prosperity theology: T. D. Jakes and the gospel of the almighty dollar.

Cross Currents (Summer) *(online)*. http://findarticles.com/p/articles/mi_m2096/is_2_57/ai_n27361438. (Accessed October 2008).

Leonard, P. (2006). *Music of a thousand hammers: Inside Habitat for Humanity*. New York: Continuum.

Ley, D. (1974). The city and good and evil: Reflections on Christian and Marxist interpretations. *Antipode, 6*(1), 66–74.

———. (2008). The immigrant church as an urban service hub. *Urban Studies, 45*(10), 2057–74.

Lienesch, M. (1993). *Redeeming America: Piety and politics in the New Christian Right*. Chapel Hill, N.C.: University of North Carolina Press.

Lindsay, D. M. (2007). *Faith in the halls of power: How evangelicals joined the American elite*. Oxford: Oxford University Press.

Lipsitz, G. (2006). Learning from New Orleans: The social warrant of hostile privatism and competitive consumer citizenship. *Cultural Anthropology, 21*(3), 451–68.

Liu, Q. (2007). How to improve government performance? *European Journal of Political Economy, 23*(4), 1198–1206.

Los Angeles Times. (2009). Obama upholds Bush faith policy. February 6. (Wallsten, P., & Helfand, D.). *(Online)*. http://articles.latimes.com/2009/feb/06/nation/na-obama-faith6. (Accessed July 2011).

Luchenitser, A. (2002). Casting aside the Constitution: The trend toward government funding of religious social service providers. *Clearinghouse Review, 615*(9/10), 615–28.

Marsden, G. (1987). *Reforming fundamentalism: Fuller Seminary and the new Evangelicalism*. Grand Rapids: William B. Eerdmans.

Martin, W. (1996). *With God on our side: The rise of the Religious Right in America*. New York: Broadway Books.

Massing, M. (1992). The tragedy of American compassion—book reviews. *Washington Monthly, 24*(9), 59–60.

Matthews, M. (1995). Let charities do welfare. *Christianity Today, 39*(5), 7.

Mead, L. (1997). *The new paternalism: Supervisory approaches to poverty*. Washington, D.C.: Brookings Institution Press.

———. (2003). A biblical response to poverty. In M. J. Bane & L. Mead (Eds.), *Lifting up the poor: A dialogue on religion, poverty and welfare reform*. (pp. 53–106). Washington, D.C.: Brookings Institution Press.

Meier, G. (1993). The new political economy and policy reform. *Journal of International Development, 5*(4), 381–89.

Mitchell, K. (2001). Transnationalism, neo-liberalism, and the rise of the shadow state. *Economy and Society, 30*(2), 165–89.

———. (2004) *Crossing the neoliberal line: Pacific Rim migration and the metropolis*. Philadelphia: Temple University Press.

Montgomery, M., & Bean, R. (1999). Market failure, government failure, and the private supply of public goods: The case of climate-controlled walkway networks. *Public Choice, 99*(3/4), 403–37.

Moore, A. (1998). After the revolution: Churches step in where welfare leaves off. *Christianity Today, 42*(14), 3.

Nagel, C. (1998). Habitat for Humanity International. In W. van Vliet (Ed.), *The encyclopedia of housing*, (pp. 206). Thousand Oaks, Calif.: Sage.

NAE (National Association of Evangelicals). (2009). About us. *National Association of Evangelicals Website (online)*. http://www.nae.net/. (Accessed June 2009).

National Association of Evangelicals Archives. (1958a). *Aid to sectarian education.* Public Policy Resolution.

———. (1958b, 1960, 1961, 1962, 1963, 1965). *Communism*. Public Policy Resolution.

———. (1964). *Church and state separation*. Public Policy Resolution.

———. (1973a). *Abortion* . Public Policy Resolution.

———. (1973b). *Federal budget*. Public Policy Resolution.

———. (1978a). *Fiscal responsibility*. Public Policy Resolution.

———. (1978b, 1984). *Fiscal responsibility*. Public Policy Resolution.

———. (1979). *Charitable contributions*. Public Policy Resolution.

———. (1980). *The Christian and his government*. Public Policy Resolution.

———. (1982). *Family*. Public Policy Resolution.

———. (1988). *AIDS*. Public Policy Resolution.

———. (1997). *Heeding the call of the poor*. Public Policy Resolution.

———. (1998). *Housing for the least of these*. Public Policy Resolution.

———. (1999). *Economic and cultural renewal*. Public Policy Resolution.

———. (2000). *Charitable Choice*. Public Policy Resolution.

———. (2003). *Faith-Based Initiative*. Public Policy Resolution.

———. (2004). *For the health of a nation*. Public Policy Resolution.

New Orleans Times-Picayune. (2007a). Sour note: Credit problems are keeping many musicians out of the Musician's Village. January 2. (Reckdahl, K.).

———. (2007b). Habitat shows musicians the way home. January 5. (Lee, A.).

New York Times. (1998). A mitzvah called Habitat for Humanity. June 21. (Liotta, J.).

———. (2000). Efforts to restrict sprawl find new resistance from advocates for affordable housing. December 25. (Oppel, R. A.).

———. (2005). Habitat for Humanity picks new leader amid turmoil. *New York Times*. August 5. (Strom, S.).

———. (2007a). Religious groups reap federal aid for pet projects. May 13. (Henriques, D., & Lehren, A.).

———. (2007b) A challenge to New York City's homeless policy. September 4. (L. Kaufman).

———. (2010). Poll finds Tea Party backers wealthier and more educated. April 14. (Zernike, K., & Thee-Brenan, M.).

NOAHH (New Orleans Area Habitat for Humanity). (2009). Current projects. *New*

Orleans Habitat for Humanity Website (online). http://www.habitat-nola.org/projects/index.php. (Accessed June 2009).

Noll, M. (2006). Where we are and how we got here. *Christianity Today, 50*(10), 42.

NORM (New Orleans Rescue Mission). (2009). Services. *New Orleans Rescue Mission Website (online).* http://www.neworleansmission.org/. (Accessed June 2009).

Obama, B. (1995). *Dreams from my father: A story of race and inheritance.* New York: Times Books.

Olasky, M. (1992). *Tragedy of American compassion.* Washington: Regnery Gateway.

———. (2000). *Compassionate conservatism: What it is, what it does, and how it can transform America.* New York: Free Press.

———. (2002). Foreword. In A. Bonner (author), *Enacted Christianity: Evangelical rescue missions in the United States and Canada* (pp. 9). Philadelphia: Xlibris.

Olree, A. (2006). *The choice principle: The biblical case for legal toleration.* New York: University Press of America.

Osteen, J. (2004). *Your best life now: 7 steps to living at your full potential.* Nashville: FaithWords.

———. (2007). *Become a better you: 7 keys to improving your life every day.* New York: Free Press.

Pacione, M. (1990). The ecclesiastical community of interest as a response to urban poverty and deprivation. *Transactions of the Institute of British Geographers, 15*(2), 193–204.

Pappu, S. (2006). The preacher. *Atlantic Monthly, 297*(2), 92–103.

Parsley, R. (2006). *Silent no more: Bringing moral clarity to America . . . while freedom still rings.* Lake Mary, Fla.: Charisma House.

Peck, J. (2006a). Liberating the city: Between New York and New Orleans. *Urban Geography, 27*(8), 681–713.

———. (2006b). Neoliberal hurricane: Who framed New Orleans? In L. Panitch & C. Leys (Eds.), *Socialist register 2007: Coming to terms with nature* (pp. 102–29). London: Merlin Press.

———. (2008). Remaking laissez-faire. *Progress in Human Geography, 32*(1), 3–43.

Peck, J., & Tickell, A. (2002). Neoliberalizing space. *Antipode, 34*(3), 380–404.

Peet, R. (2003). *Unholy trinity: The IMF, World Bank, and WTO.* Boston: Zed Press.

Pew Forum. (2011). The Tea Party and religion: Analysis. (February 23) *(online).* http://pewforum.org/Politics-and-Elections/Tea-Party-and-Religion.aspx. (Accessed June 23, 2011).

Polanyi, K. (1944). *The great transformation.* London: Victor Gollancz.

Phillips, K. (2006). *American theocracy: The peril and politics of radical religion, oil, and borrowed money in the 21st century.* New York: Penguin.

Rand, A. (1943). *The Fountainhead.* Indianapolis: Bobbs-Merrill.

———. (1957). *Atlas Shrugged.* New York: Random House.

Reckford, J. (2007). *Creating a habitat for humanity: No hands but yours.* Minneapolis, Minn.: Fortress Press.

Reingold, D., Pirog, M., & Brady, B. (2007). Empirical evidence on faith-based organizations in an era of welfare reform. *Social Service Review, 81*(2), 245–83.

Reisman, D. A. (1998). Adam Smith on market and state. *Journal of Institutional and Theoretical Economics, 154*(2), 1–383.

Richards, J. (2009). *Money, greed, and God: Why capitalism is the solution and not the problem*. New York: Harper One.

Rothbard, M. (1980). Myth and truth about libertarianism. *Modern Age, 24*(1), 9–15.

———. (2006). The origins of individualist anarchism in the U.S. *Daily Article* (February 1) *(online)*. http://www.mises.org/story/2014. (Accessed October 2008).

Rudin, J. (2006). *The baptizing of America: The Religious Right's plans for the rest of us*. New York: Thunder's Mouth Press.

Sager, R. (2006). *The elephant in the room: Evangelicals, libertarians, and the battle to control the Republican Party*. Hoboken, N.J.: John Wiley and Sons.

Samuelson, P. (1954). The pure theory of public expenditure. *Review of Economics and Statistics, 36*(4), 387–89.

Schaeffer, F. (1982). *A Christian manifesto*. Westchester, Ill.: Crossway Books.

Schansberg, E. (2005). Afterthoughts on the aftermath of the New Orleans flood. *Acton Institute Commentary Website* (October 5) *(online)*. http://www.acton.org/commentary/commentary_290.php. (Accessed May 2009).

Schwartz, A. (2006). *Housing policy in the United States: An introduction*. New York: Routledge.

Sekou, O. (2008). Whose God?: Faith, democracy, and the making of an authentic religious Left. In F. Clarkson (Ed.), *Dispatches from the Religious Left* (pp. 61–78). New York: IG.

Sherman, A. (1999). How Sharon Baptist discovered welfare ministry. *Christianity Today, 43*(7), 78–81.

Sider, R., & Knippers, D. (2005). Introduction. In R. Sider & D. Knippers (Eds.), *Toward an evangelical public policy: Political strategies for the health of a nation*. Grand Rapids, Mich.: Baker Books.

Smith, C. (1998). *American Evangelicalism: Embattled and thriving*. Chicago: University of Chicago Press.

Smith, S. R., & Sosin, M. R. (2001). Varieties of faith-related agencies. *Public Administration Review, 61*(6), 651–70.

Spain, D. (2001). Redemptive places, Charitable Choice, and welfare reform. *Journal of the American Planning Association, 67*(3), 249–62.

Staeheli, L., Kodras, J., & Flint, C. (Eds.). (1997). *State devolution in America: Implications for a diverse society*. Thousand Oaks, Calif.: Sage.

State of Louisiana. (2009). Department of Social Services, homeless shelters: A–Z. *State of Louisiana Website (online)*. http://www.dss.state.la.us/index.cfm?md=pagebuilder&tmp=home&pid=207. (Accessed December 2009).

Steinberg, R. (1991). Does government spending crowd out donations? Interpreting the evidence. *Annals of Public and Cooperative Economics, 62*(4), 591–617.

Sugg, J. (2005). A nation under God. *Mother Jones* (December/January) *(online).* http://www.motherjones.com/news/feature/2005/12/a_nation_under_god.html. (Accessed October 2008).

Suskind, Ron. (2003). Why are these men laughing? *Esquire Magazine* (January 1). http://www.esquire.com/features/ESQ0103-JAN_ROVE_rev_2. (Accessed September 2011).

Sziarto, K. (2008). Placing legitimacy: Organizing religious support in a hospital workers' contract campaign. *Tijdschrift voor Economische en Sociale Geografie, 99*(4), 406–25.

Tapia, A. (1994). Urban relocators building bridges. *Christianity Today, 38*(10), 50–51.

Taylor, J., & Van Doren, P. (2005). The case against the strategic petroleum reserve. *Policy Analysis No. 555.* CATO Institute: 1–24.

Toronto Star. (1993). "I'm just a carpenter": Former president Jimmy Carter leads 700 volunteers in building new houses for needy families at Habitat for Humanity sites. July 24.

———. (1995). Family's house seeking a home bungalow built by volunteers being stored in parking lot. April 4. (Welsh, M.).

———. (2002a). Building hope: The Star to join with Habitat in project during Pope's visit. March 30. (Cordileone, E.).

———. (2002b). City strike stalls housing project—Habitat homes for poor families put on hold. August 19. (Orchard, R.).

———. (2002c). Habitat venture a natural—GTHBA, builders pitching in at Home Show to help build housing for the needy. April 6. (Libfeld, S.).

———. (2002d). Home at last—barrier-free Habitat for Humanity home will allow couple to finally marry and live under the same roof. July 20. (Teotonio, I).

———. (2002e). Why Habitat for Humanity builds more than just homes. July 25. (Orchard, R.).

———. (2004). A new floor for a new life. September 13. (Fiorita, J.).

———. (2005a). Christmas cheers in new townhouse home for the holidays. December 24. (Teotonio, I.).

———. (2005b). Singles pair up for Habitat build. February 10.

———. (2006). All work, some play. January 28. (Crew, R.).

———. (2007). Project helps needy families enter housing market. January 6. (Greer, S.).

Trigg, R., & Nabangi, F. K. (1995). Representations of the financial position of non-profit organizations: The Habitat for Humanity situation. *Financial Accountability and Management, 11*(3), 259–69.

Trudeau, D. (2008). Junior partner or empowered community? The role of nonprofit social service providers amidst state restructuring. *Urban Studies, 45*(13), 2805–27.

Twombly, E. (2002). Religious versus secular human service organizations: Implications for public policy. *Social Science Quarterly, 83*(4), 947–61.

U.S. Census Bureau. (2006). *State and Metropolitan Area Data Book*. http://www.census.gov/compendia/smadb/. (Accessed September 2011).

———. (2008). *City and County Data Book*. U.S. Census Bureau. http://www.census.gov/statab/www/ccdb.html. (Accessed September 2011).

U.S. Conference of Mayors. (2007). *A status report on hunger and homelessness in America's cities: A 23-city survey*. Washington, D.C.: U.S. Conference of Mayors. Research report.

Van Biema, D., & Chu, J. (2006). Does God want you to be rich? *Time Magazine* (September 18) *(online)*. http://www.time.com/time/magazine/article/0,9171,1533448,00.html. (Accessed October 2008).

Wallis, J., & Dollery, B. (2002). Wolf's model: Government failure and public sector reform in advanced industrial democracies. *Review of Policy Research, 19*(1), 177–203.

Wall Street Journal. (1987). Tapping the shadow housing market. March 13. (Postrel, V.).

———. (1995). Government endangers a Habitat for volunteers. July 11. (Husock, H.).

———. (2002). Habitat project gives U.S. firms dose of goodwill. August 28. (Kopecki, D.).

———. (2006). Privatize the welfare state. March 9. (Husock, H.).

Washington Times. (1995). Woman works way into home—Habitat for Humanity assists families with jobs and willingness to labor. July 8. (Tate, S.).

Weber, M. (1958) [1905]. *The Protestant ethic and the spirit of capitalism*. New York: Scribner.

———. (2004). Introduction to the economic ethics of the world religions. In S. Whimster (Ed.), *The Essential Weber* (pp. 55–80). London: Routledge.

White House Office of the Press Secretary. (2009). Obama announces White House Office of faith-based and neighborhood partnerships. *White House Website* (February 5) *(online)*. http://www.whitehouse.gov/the_press_office/ObamaAnnouncesWhiteHouseOfficeofFaith-basedandNeighborhoodPartnerships/. (Accessed July 2010).

Wilcox, C., & Larson, C. (2006). *Onward Christian soldiers: The Religious Right in American politics*. Boulder, Colo.: Westview Press.

Williams, A. (2005). Dominionist fantasies. *Frontpage Magazine* (May 4) *(online)*. http://www.frontpagemagazine.com/Articles/Read.aspx?GUID=86BEC0B4-D01C-40A0-A060-33D9FB999057. (Accessed October 2008).

Willis, G. (2006). *What Jesus meant*. New York: Viking.

Wilson, D. (2004). Toward a contingent urban neoliberalism. *Urban Geography, 25*(8), 771–83.

Wilson, E. (1996). Saving the safety net. *Christianity Today, 40*(8), 25.

Winner, L. (1999). 84,000 join Jakes in Georgia. *Christianity Today, 44*(2) *(online)*. http://www.christianitytoday.com/ct/1999/september6/9ta23a.html. (Accessed September 2011).

Winston, C. (2000). Government failure in urban transportation. *Fiscal Studies, 21*(4), 403–25.

Wolfe, A. (2003). *The transformation of American religion: How we actually live our faith*. New York: Free Press.

Wuthnow, R. (2004). *Saving America?: Faith-based services and the future of civil society*. Princeton, N.J.: Princeton University Press.

Ziegler, J. (2005). Testimony to subcommittee on human resources of the House Committee on ways and means on February 10, 2005. *U.S. House of Representatives Website (online)*. http://waysandmeans.house.gov/hearings.asp?formmode=view&id=2969. (Accessed October 2006).

INDEX

GEOGRAPHIES OF JUSTICE AND SOCIAL TRANSFORMATION

1. *Social Justice and the City*, rev. ed.
   by David Harvey
2. *Begging as a Path to Progress: Indigenous Women and Children and the Struggle for Ecuador's Urban Spaces*
   by Kate Swanson
3. *Making the San Fernando Valley: Rural Landscapes, Western Heritage, and White Privilege*
   by Laura R. Barraclough
4. *Company Towns in the Americas: Landscape, Power, and Working-Class Communities*
   edited by Oliver J. Dinius and Angela Vergara
5. *Tremé: Race and Place in a New Orleans Neighborhood*
   by Michael E. Crutcher Jr.
6. *Bloomberg's New York: Class and Governance in the Luxury City*
   by Julian Brash
7. *Roppongi Crossing: The Demise of a Tokyo Nightclub District and the Reshaping of a Global City*
   by Roman Adrian Cybriwsky
8. *Fitzgerald: Geography of a Revolution*
   by William Bunge
9. *Accumulating Insecurity: Violence and Dispossession in the Making of Everyday Life*
   edited by Shelley Feldman, Charles Geisler, and Gayatri A. Menon
10. *They Saved the Crops: Labor, Landscape, and the Struggle over Industrial Farming in Bracero-Era California*
    by Don Mitchell
11. *Faith Based: Religious Neoliberalism and the Politics of Welfare in the United States*
    by Jason Hackworth

CPSIA information can be obtained
at www.ICGtesting.com
Printed in the USA
FFOW02n2138141214
9545FF